<u>S</u>ky Woman Lives in Me

ROBERTA CAPASSO

9-10-16

Lucretia,

Thank you for reading this book!

Sincerely,

Roberta Capasso

ISBN: 978-1-4834-4348-5 (sc)
ISBN: 978-1-4834-4346-1 (hc)
ISBN: 978-1-4834-4347-8 (e)

Library of Congress Control Number: 2015920547

Because of the dynamic nature of the Internet, any web addresses or links contained in this book may have changed since publication and may no longer be valid. The views expressed in this work are solely those of the author and do not necessarily reflect the views of the publisher, and the publisher hereby disclaims any responsibility for them.

Any people depicted in stock imagery provided by Thinkstock are models, and such images are being used for illustrative purposes only. Certain stock imagery © Thinkstock.

Lulu Publishing Services rev. date: 2/5/2016

I dedicate this book to the memory of Elizabeth Hill-Huff-Denny, my great-great-grandmother; Sophia Huff-Powless, my great-grandmother; and Mildred Henrietta Powless-Elm, my Grandma Millie. I also dedicate this book to a new generation, my sons, Michael and Patrick, so they can learn and share this story with future generations. This book is also dedicated to the thousands of Native American Indians, of past and present generations, who weren't allowed to be brought up in their native culture and language or to know who they truly are.

Contents

Foreword

My wife did not wake up one morning and decide to write a story about her Native American ancestors. Instead, this project evolved over thirteen years, beginning in 2000 when she saw the picture of her great-great-grandmother, Elizabeth Hill-Huff-Denny in her sister Sherry's house. That spark set my wife on fire to learn about her family and her Native American heritage. Little did she know at the time that it was also the advent of her own self-discovery.

The decision to provide our children with a printed archive on their Native American ancestors came years later. In June 2003, my wife, Bobbie, and I first visited the grounds of the Indian Industrial Boarding School in Carlisle, Pennsylvania, which are now home to the US Army War College. She wanted to see where her great-grandmother Sophia Huff went to school. Three years of research, including trips to the Oneida Indian Reservation near Green Bay, Wisconsin, and University of Wisconsin–Green Bay Research Center; interviews with family and tribal elders; and contacts with the Milwaukee Public Museum Anthropology Department staff and the Oneida Indian Language Department, had brought us to this moment.

As I looked upon the US Army War College buildings and surroundings, I thought, *So here's where Jim Thorpe played football!* I envisioned a place where Native American children embraced a modern-day equivalent of a vocational school experience—a place where something good happened.

My wife's perspective was much different. She was keenly aware of the disturbing events in Native American history that led to Sophia's trip here in 1891. That history is worthy of further discussion, but it's beyond the scope of what you're about to read.

For Bobbie, walking the grounds for the first time was somewhat shocking. Part of that reaction came from her realization that she was a direct descendant of someone who had actually been here in 1891, and most of it came from her simply trying to digest what it might have been like to live here back then. Curiosity finally triumphed over concern, although she was aware of some of the abuses Sophia had endured while attending Carlisle.

The second visit to Carlisle in 2010 was more sobering. The previous seven years of research had not made my wife dizzy with joy. Painful discoveries about the lives and times of Elizabeth, Sophia, Lily, and the Oneida people continued to mount. The picture was becoming clearer and her epiphany accelerated. The culture and way of life that Elizabeth and Sophia had inherited was being extinguished. Sophia and Lily were sent to Carlisle to be assimilated—to be stripped of anything Indian. And sadly, Bobbie had become what Elizabeth and Sophia resisted so strongly: an Oneida on the outside and an assimilated white on the inside. Our drive home from Carlisle was memorable. My wife had moments of outrage, pain, and humiliation. It was as if we had just left a crime scene, but instead of Sophia being the victim, paradoxically, my wife now realized her own victimization.

That was it! The true story about this one Native America Indian family's heritage would be told. She was committed to fully sharing this story. It would reflect her own raw emotions that had erupted after decades of neglect. She was going to follow the facts wherever they led her; a dark chapter in this nation's history would be viewed in a new light.

One evening I came home to find my wife quite angry after reading about the Burke Act of 1906. This US government policy was particularly destructive to Native American families, land ownership, and tribal autonomy. So when I jokingly asked her if she was going to kill me and all Euro-Americans, she said no. After a pregnant pause, she said, "But the politicians who made this law, maybe."

The story of General Richard Henry Pratt and his role in establishing an off-reservation boarding school for Native American children further energized Bobbie in her work. Many well-intentioned Euro-Americans in the late 1800s mistakenly believed Native Americans to be savages whose only hope for survival was rapid assimilation into the white culture. Pratt believed that his "Kill the Indian, Save the Man" educational experiment would lead to a better future for Native Americans. Indeed there were some success stories, but at what price? For my wife, Elizabeth, Sophia, and for many Native American families, the cost was dear.

So how profound was the impact of the life of Sophia Huff on this one living descendant of hers? It all bubbled over when we first visited the Tomlinson house, where Sophia had worked as a servant and lived for ten years, from 1892 until 1902. Bobbie trembled with emotion as the Johnson family, current owners of this property, graciously welcomed us into their home for a tour. She bit her lip to keep herself from bursting into tears. It was the emotional crucible that forged her transformation and propelled her on to write this story.

The story about to unfold is important in many ways. It is a story about our children's great-great-great-grandmother and her daughter, who were born in the 1800s. It's a story about their Native American Indian heritage and what these two women did to preserve it. It is also a story about a people's sorrow and celebration, despair and salvation, and the triumph of the human spirit over ignorance, arrogance, and bigotry.

Equally important, it is also my wife's story of rebirth and self-discovery. In the Oneida story of creation, Sky Woman lands safely on the back of a turtle. Three clans of Oneida people subsequently evolved: the Wolf, the Bear, and the Turtle. The people of the Turtle Clan are considered keepers of the land and the well of information. Those on the matriarchal side of Bobbie's family are descendants of the Turtle Clan. When Bobbie was seven years old, a picture of her ancestor in the museum spoke to her and led her to a new awareness of the Oneida that runs through her.

Sky Woman Lives in Me is also a challenge to all of us. It is a warning, a reminder, a humble proclamation of what can happen if we forget our past. Ask Jewish Americans why they remember the Holocaust. Ask African Americans why Martin Luther King Day is important to all Americans. Maybe someday there will a be a National Day of Remembrance for Native American Indians like Sophia Huff, poor in worldly possession and social status but rich in dignity, spirit, and resolve.

Our children and their descendants have their family heirlooms; my wife deserves all the credit. Her work has inspired me and other readers to better cherish our heritage while embracing the diversity of cultures across the world. For me personally, the story of Sophia Huff and Elizabeth Hill is a reminder to remain humble when conducting my affairs and to never forget that all people are equal in the eyes of their Creator.

By Charles "Chick" Capasso

Acknowledgments

Many people have helped me learn about my Oneida Indian heritage. My research has taken around thirteen years. It is still ongoing, for I never want to stop learning about my heritage. Learning about my background has been a real eye-opener for me. It has been a long journey through years of research. It has been a heartfelt, wonderful discovery of who I really am.

From the bottom of my heart, I sincerely thank my husband, Charles "Chick" Capasso, for all the support and help he gave me during these past thirteen years. His encouragement has given me the confidence to research and write this story. I also thank him for writing the foreword.

I thank Mary Sherman and Mike Valentino for editing my manuscript. They both have been so helpful to me in writing and telling my story clearly.

I am grateful to the following people who read my manuscript during its evolution and gave me their honest comments and helpful feedback: Charles "Chick" Capasso, Mike Capasso, Pat Capasso, Alli Capasso, John Rahn, Ann Sechrist, Sadie Gilbertson, R. A. Guirand, Rhonda Clancey, Linda Roberts and Allegra Roberts, Felicia and Barry Bernhardt, and Erica San Dretto.

I am extremely thankful to Barb Smith and her son Geoff for helping me find out where Sophia Huff lived in New Jersey for ten years. The history they provided about their outing students, including Grace

Thumbo, was so important and much appreciated. Sincere thanks to Mary and Bob Tomlinson as well for their Tomlinson Family Genealogy.

Thank you to Barb Landis, researcher of the Carlisle Indian Industrial School and historian at the Cumberland County Historical Society. Barb took my husband and me on a tour of what used to be the Carlisle Schools grounds. Interviewing her about the school was very helpful, and she provided excellent feedback upon reading an earlier draft of my story. She has been a tremendous help to me on my book.

I have to thank Ken and Sandy Johnson and their sons, Chris, Nick, and Kevin, and dog, Junior, for allowing me to tour the house my great-grandma Sophia lived in for ten years as a servant. I was overcome with emotion upon finding and seeing this house, and its memory still fills me with emotion.

Thank you to the Oneida Nation Cultural Center; Oneida Language Department; the University of Wisconsin–Green Bay Research Center; Holy Apostles Episcopal Church in Oneida, Wisconsin; the Milwaukee Public Museum Anthropology Department; the National Archives and Records Administration in Washington, DC; the Camden County Historical Society in New Jersey; and the Cumberland County Historical Society in Carlisle, Pennsylvania. I thank Dr. Nancy Lurie for her advice.

I also sincerely thank Barb Skenandore for her Oneida history and genealogy expertise. Ancestry.com was very helpful, as was the National Archives and Research Center (NARA) located in Washington, DC.

Although they are no longer with us, my sincerest gratitude goes to my great-grandmother Sophia Josephine Huff-Powless and her mother, Elizabeth Hill-Huff-Denny. Women hold a place of high honor and respect in the Oneida culture. I learned the Oneida are very matriarchal. I felt Elizabeth's and Sophia's presence many times over the past thirteen years. I still do. It is these two women who have made this story possible.

My heartfelt thanks also go to my grandma Millie, Mildred H. Elm, for sharing stories of her mother, Sophia, with me over the years. Her stories helped me understand why I hadn't known who I really am. I now see the Oneida inside me and am grateful and proud of it.

To everyone mentioned above who gave me words of encouragement, thank you! This story of my discovery of my Native American heritage is but one of many similar still untold stories of Native American ancestry across the United States. Today, many Native Americans across our country wonder why they look Native American Indian but act white. They know nothing of their Indian ancestry, like I did. Our stories must be told so that everyone can know the real, honest, untold history of the Native American Indians. Our school books never discussed what really happened to us. My book does!

Thank you also to all my relatives and Oneida elders who provided information about Sophia, Elizabeth, and the Oneida Indians here in Wisconsin.

Above all, I thank God, our Creator, for the people and events that helped me. Now I can share my Oneida heritage with my sons and nieces and nephews, and generations to come.

Introduction

I never thought I would write a book after seeing a photo of an old Indian lady I didn't know displayed in the Milwaukee Public Museum when I was seven, and I didn't expect that I'd think about this old lady for decades. It was really spooky, then, when I came across this photo again in the year 2000—and learned we were relatives! How had I never known that this old lady, Elizabeth Hill-Huff-Denny, and I were relatives? Never did I expect to spend thirteen long years researching why another relative of mine, Sophie Josephine Huff-Powless, spent eleven years out east: one year at the Carlisle Indian Industrial Boarding School and ten years working and living with a Quaker family. Why was Sophia taken away from her family and home at fourteen and a half? Why had this Quaker family become her family? The fact that I looked Oneida Indian but didn't know anything about Oneida Indians bothered me for years. Why did I look Oneida on the outside but I identified myself as white on the inside? A part of me seemed to be missing. Why was I prejudiced against my Indian self? Why had reservations been set up across the United States for Native Americans? Why had the Carlisle Indian School been established?

Elizabeth was my great-great-grandmother, and Sophia was my great-grandmother. Both of these ladies were Oneida Indian. They were part of the Turtle Clan. Turtle Clan members like Elizabeth and Sophia were the keepers of the land. They also provided the well of information of the Oneida culture to others in the tribe. My desire to learn about these two ladies and to know the answers to the questions presented above changed my life forever. Elizabeth and Sophia shared their knowledge with me as I researched their lives. It almost seemed spiritual. No longer would I be another assimilated Native American Indian adrift and disconnected from my true identity.

The pain and suffering that my ancestors endured entered my soul unfiltered for the first time. It was sobering in its magnitude.

Now it is my turn to enlighten you and future generations. This Turtle Clan member will tell the real story of Elizabeth and Sophia.

The Picture

In the early 1960s, I was living with my seven siblings in a run-down house on Kilbourn Avenue in Milwaukee, Wisconsin. We went to Kilbourn Avenue School, which is now a rescue mission. Our rented house and the other homes on that block have long since been condemned and demolished.

One day when I was about seven, some of my siblings and I headed out to walk to the Milwaukee Public Museum, about six blocks away. On the way, we stopped at a corner grocery store to buy some penny candy. Yes, in those days, most candy cost only a penny! I wanted to buy my favorite, a Big Time candy bar, but it cost a nickel, which I didn't have. So, with my pennies, I bought a two-pack of Chum Gum and a Tootsie Roll. Why the gum was called Chum Gum I don't know; maybe because it was a pack of two sticks, one stick for me and one stick to share, of powder-pink gum. All I know is that it only cost one cent, and it tasted good!

After buying our candy, we kept on to the museum. I can't remember what it cost each of us to get in—maybe a dime per kid? We spent hours checking out the various exhibits and displays. At that time, the museum also housed the Milwaukee Public Library. The building was huge, with impressive old stone columns at the front entrance. Today it houses only the public library, as a new museum was built behind it on Wells Street.

We gaped at the exhibits of elephants, lions, and other animals. We saw mummies in the Egyptian exhibit. There were so many exhibits to see that day. Going to the museum was a learning experience for me. I loved it. I saw a lot of different things from all over the world in one building. It seemed that the whole world and all its cultures were displayed. After looking at the mummies, we saw stuffed zebras, bears, buffalo, wolves, and so many more animals that I can't name them all. A day certainly wasn't enough for anyone to see everything there. But we took in all we could that day.

I also checked out the American Indian displays. "You are part Oneida Indian," relatives had told me. That was it. *What was that? Oneida Indian?* I wondered. Since I was only a child, I just shrugged and went on with my young life.

One exhibit had American Indian artifacts displayed behind big glass windows. I saw cradleboards, bows and arrows, baskets, buckskin clothing, beaded moccasins, Indian headdresses, and arrowheads. I had seen these items in Western movies on our black-and-white television. Another display housed a diorama showing Indians hunting buffalo on the plains, and still another diorama featured teepees and Indians sitting around a campfire. The teepees reminded me again of Western movies, and the Indians made me think about those wild Indians on TV with their painted faces screaming their lungs out and dancing around a campfire. *Boy, those Indians are savages,* I thought. I didn't know then that I was related to them.

I approached another display of black-and-white pictures of Indians. I didn't know who they were or where they were from, but one really caught my attention. I didn't know why. It was a black-and-white picture of an elderly Indian woman with snow-white hair. She was wearing dark clothes, a black shawl around her shoulders, and a dark scarf on her head. She was walking outside in the snow. For some strange reason, I could not take my eyes off this picture. It was as if the old lady wanted to get my attention. And boy did she. I didn't know her from the man in the moon, yet this picture mesmerized me. She was very small and didn't seem to be posing. I wondered why she wasn't wearing a warm coat instead of a shawl. It was snowy and must have been cold wherever she was. I wanted to give her my winter coat. It was sad to see her in just a shawl in the dead of winter, although she did look strong and independent. But she also looked lonely. Unexpectedly, the vision of this old lady stayed with me for years, flashing through my mind at odd times. I kept wondering who she was. I guess you could say she haunted me.

I didn't know her tribe or where she was from. As I think about it now, I realize that something might have been written about this on the display, but I was so taken by the picture that I really didn't notice its surroundings. I don't even remember any of the other pictures of Indians included—just this old woman trudging through the snow. Later on I learned that these black-and-white pictures were of Oneida Indians from the Oneida Indian Reservation near Green Bay, Wisconsin. I still did not know who that old lady was.

I have to admit that I really didn't know that there were many different Indian tribes in America. I thought the Indians had chosen the name "Indians." Actually, we are indigenous tribes, which mean we originated here in the Americas, and we were named Indians by Columbus, who thought he had landed in India when he arrived here. My tribe, Oneida, is one of the many tribes indigenous to the United States. I also thought a reservation was land Indians themselves had set aside to settle on. I was wrong. I had no idea that a reservation was land set aside by the US government for Indians to live on, thus making former Indian lands available for whites to settle on. As I think back, I never saw an Indian reservation until my family moved to a place way up north near Lac du Flambeau, Wisconsin, in 1966. The Indian reservation nearby was called the Chippewa Indian Reservation. I was around thirteen.

I was born in 1953 at Deaconess Hospital in downtown Milwaukee, the city where I lived my first twelve young years. Most of my siblings were born at this hospital too. Deaconess Hospital no longer is standing, having been demolished years ago, and the land where it stood is now part of the Marquette University campus. Being initially raised in Milwaukee, I was a city girl. When my family moved from a one-year stay in Greenfield, Wisconsin (a suburb of Milwaukee), to the woods of northern Wisconsin, near the Lac du Flambeau Chippewa Indian Reservation, it was a cultural shock! I'm sure it was for my siblings, too. None of us had ever seen a reservation.

On my first day of school in Lac du Flambeau, my siblings and I rode the school bus from our run-down cabin in the woods to the Lac du Flambeau Grade School, located about seven miles away. Our cabin had been a hunting shack, and an abandoned sawmill sat on the premises nearby. The house was heated only by a woodstove in the winter. I remember the linoleum floor and drafty windows, over which we put plastic sheeting to keep the house warmer in the winter. Our closest neighbor was an old man who lived in a very run-down trailer across the road from us. We called him "the hermit," as we never learned his real name. He raised a few billy goats. One time, as a joke, we brought one of the goats into our house to scare our mother. It worked!

All of us kids and our mother and stepfather shared one bathroom in our one-thousand-square-foot shack, which I hated. My four sisters and I slept in one room, and our five brothers slept in another room on the first floor. For a while, my mother and stepfather had their bed in the living room, but then we ten kids were moved to an unfinished attic with rafters showing, no ceiling, and only insulation for our walls. The floor wasn't finished, either. A wooden divider built in the middle of the attic separated the girls' sleeping quarters from the boys'. In the summer months, the attic got really hot. We also had bats that flew into the attic and down the stairs! I hated the bats, which most likely had rabies and frightened all of us. One night my sisters all screamed at me while I was asleep because a bat had gotten under my blanket. Their screams woke me up, thank God. I was so upset that I couldn't sleep the rest of that night. I sat up all that same night afraid a bat would come bother me again. My other four sisters crawled into my older sister Sue's Falcon and slept in that car the rest of that night.

When my siblings and I took the bus to school the first day, I was really shocked at what I saw near Lac du Flambeau. The school bus stopped to pick up kids who lived in "the old Indian Village of Lac du Flambeau." Indians and non-Indians alike called this rundown section of Lac du Flambeau "the old Indian Village." The newer side of town was just called Lac du Flambeau. These kids were Chippewa Indian, and this old Indian village was their home. The village was so run-down that suddenly my run-down, bats-in-the-belfry, hunting shack seemed like a palace. I was appalled to see the dilapidated homes these Chippewa Indian children come running out of to catch the bus. One home had nothing but a dirt floor—not even thin linoleum like my place. I was shocked and saddened to see this, as I had never seen such poverty before. I felt helpless. I wondered why this place was so run-down and poor. Yes, my family was poor too, but I had never witnessed such poverty as I did that day on the school bus.

After our visit to the museum, we headed back home. I kept thinking about that old lady in the picture, but I didn't say anything about it to my siblings. I was baffled by my attraction to it. When we arrived home, I still didn't share that I felt sad that that lady didn't have a warmer coat and that she looked cold and lonely. After that day, I never forgot this picture of this old woman.

Years later, in May 2000 to be exact, I drove up to visit my sister Sherry and her husband, Joel, in De Pere, Wisconsin. Sherry showed me around her home. On the wall in one room hung a bunch of framed black-and-white pictures. Sherry pointed at each one and told me about it, and all of a sudden I noticed one that really surprised me. There on her wall hung that same picture I had seen in the Milwaukee Public Museum in the early 1960s as a seven-year-old! There was the old lady with snow-white hair wrapped in her black shawl and scarf walking outside in the winter. I was shocked.

I immediately asked Sherry, "Where did you get this picture from? Why is this picture hanging on your wall?"

Sherry looked at me and said, "Bobbie, this old lady is our great-great-grandmother!"

"What?" I said.

"This old lady is Elizabeth Hill, our great-great-grandmother."

"We are related to this old woman? How do you know this? When did you find this out?"

Sherry told me that she had found out about this old lady from our grandma Millie. In fact, Grandma Millie had a copy of this same picture and other pictures of Elizabeth Hill in a photo album. I was really surprised to learn that this elderly Oneida Indian woman was related to me, after all these years that the picture had haunted my mind. To this day I am startled by how firmly this picture had been etched in my mind and for how long. Now, at almost fifty years old, I had learned who she was, Elizabeth Hill-Huff-Denny, my great-great-grandmother. Wow!

As I looked at the picture on Sherry's wall, I felt somewhat disappointed that none of my relatives had said anything about Elizabeth before now—nothing about her picture being displayed in the museum or about our relation to her. And oddly, my siblings' and my elder relatives knew about this picture being displayed in the museum and had actually seen it on display themselves. I was confused by this. After seeing this picture again, I knew I had to find out more about this old lady and why our elder relatives had never told us about her. Sherry sent me a copy of this picture, which I still cherish today, and I embarked on a mission to learn more about this tiny woman, Elizabeth Hill-Huff-Denny, my great-great-grandmother.

I contacted the Milwaukee Public Museum's Anthropology Department to find out more about this picture and the display in general. I learned that these photos were displayed to show museum visitors what Oneida Indians from the Oneida Indian Reservation near Green Bay, Wisconsin, looked like. The only Indians I had seen before my visit to the museum at seven years old were the Indians on television in cowboy movies, so this image of Elizabeth—without feathers in her hair, without a buckskin dress or moccasins—hadn't registered as an image of an Indian.

My family never discussed our Oneida Indian heritage when I was growing up, and I really didn't know I was Indian for years, and even then I was told only that I was Oneida Indian. That was it! I really don't know how much my elder relatives knew about their Oneida heritage either.

When I was a kid in the '50s, and even before I was born, it was taboo to share your Native American heritage. Even at age sixty in the year 2013, I was shocked to learn that sharing my Oneida Heritage with me when I was a child was frowned upon by the U.S. Government. But, I learned through talking to elders in my family and through historical research that the US government wanted all Indians, even future generations, assimilated into white European culture.[1] To me, it seems the government didn't consider Native Americans human. Indians were considered savages and our culture unacceptable; thus, we had to be assimilated into white culture to be saved from our savagery and be considered human.[2] It tore at my heart to learn this. No wonder I had never been allowed to know anything about being Native American Indian! Because of the decree that required the assimilation of Indians into white culture made by the US government in the late nineteenth century, I was allowed only to look Indian—red on the outside—and was required to grow up white inside, having no clue about my true heritage. This was also why I also wasn't able to share my Indian heritage with anyone, including my own children. But, as you'll learn as my story continues, the Indian that shows on the outside of me is also within me now.

So who was Elizabeth Hill-Huff-Denny? After doing research about her these past thirteen years, I wish I had met her and known her. I would've loved to have talked Oneida to her and shared her stories with family and friends. In my heart I know I would probably have learned a lot about my Oneida heritage from her. I also would've loved to have gotten to know Sophia Huff-Powless, Elizabeth's daughter, better too. But because of the taboo and US government restrictions against teaching Oneida culture to younger generations, my learning the history of Elizabeth and Sophia was forbidden. The Oneida language also wasn't allowed to be spoken or taught to subsequent Native American Indian generations by our elders. Being Native American Indian from any tribe was not allowed. I was denied my Native American culture. But no longer! I am ready to share what I've learned about myself and my heritage. This is a history lesson I am still learning about so I can share more with everyone, especially future generations of Native American Indians.

On the next page (fig. 1) is the picture I saw displayed in the Milwaukee Public Museum as a seven-year-old in the early 1960s. I didn't know then that this lady, Elizabeth Hill-Huff-Denny, was my great-great-grandmother! Now I know who she is, and I want to share this with you.

Figure 1-This is the photo of my Great-great Grandmother, Elizabeth Hill-Huff-Denny displayed in the early 1960s in the Milwaukee Public Museum. Courtesy Milwaukee Public Museum Anthropology Department.

Elizabeth Hill-Huff-Denny

I had to go way back in family history and census records to learn about Elizabeth. In the 1820s, as children, her parents were forced to come to Wisconsin from New York.[3] They were born on Oneida Indian land in upstate New York and had been given Oneida Indian names. I do not know what those names were, but I sure wish I did. The US government changed their names to Antone and Esther Hill, as part of the policy that promoted assimilation of Indians into the white, European culture in the 1800s. Actual Indian names were never recorded again. This name changing totally shocked and outraged me. I couldn't help but think about Kunta Kinte's name being changed to Toby in the novel *Roots*. In the story, Kunta had to have a white name …his African heritage was to be erased.[4] I see this as discrimination against who Kunte really was—and the changing of Antone, Esther and Elizabeth's names from their Oneida names was also discriminatory.

The US government wanted to make New York Oneida Indian lands available to non-Indian settlers to live on. Thus, it moved Oneida Indians, including Antone and Esther Hill, off of their homelands and gave these lands away to white settlers forever! Some Oneida were moved to Canada, and others were moved to Wisconsin and given land originally owned by the Menominee and Winnebago Indian tribes. This land was renamed the Oneida Indian Reservation of Wisconsin.[5] Antone, Esther, and other Oneida ancestors' forced move was a real shock to me, and that Indian lands across the entire United States were being made available for non-Indian immigrants to settle on—and Indians being moved off their lands to government-established reservations across America—appalled me. As a child, I had thought reservations were lands set aside by Indians themselves for themselves! I now know I was wrong.

For the Oneidas forced to move to Wisconsin, the land they were given, near Duck Creek and Green Bay, was decent at that time. However, I was appalled that the amount of land given to the Oneidas in Wisconsin in the 1820s was much smaller than promised. Two treaties the federal government signed with the Menominee and Ho Chunk Nations in 1821 and 1822 specified the reservation of millions of acres from just north of Milwaukee south and west to the Fox River and Lake Winnebago and north to the Straits of Mackinac. But the Menominee later contested these two treaties, thus further reducing the amount of land to be given to the Oneidas. By the 1830s, the Oneida's access to 500,000 acres dwindled to just over 65,400 acres. Today the 65,400 acres still is Oneida land, with its only access via Duck Creek, near Green Bay. The Oneida Reservation featured plenty of timber, fish, and game to hunt and farmland at that time. This was in contrast to other Native American tribes. Their land was poor in resources and tough to survive on. This saddened me.

Yes, the Oneida Reservation was much smaller than promised, but in the 1820s, it was habitable enough for Oneidas to make a living on, making my Oneida tribe luckier than most Indians in our country at that time.

The Episcopal Church of New York State and the US government moved Antone and Esther here in the 1820s. Episcopal Minister Eleazer Williams helped move the initial group of Oneida, and it was discovered that he had received money from New York State, the US government, and the Ogden Land Company to move the Oneida.[6] When I learned this I lost all respect for Reverend Williams, the federal government, and the Ogden Land Company, for the resettlement had been only about the land and money. Later on the Methodist Church of New York State also helped the US government move another group of Oneidas to the reservation in Wisconsin, and both the Methodist Church and the Episcopal Church served as caretakers and Christian missionaries there. Both of these churches had received government money to help resettle the Oneidas there. I feel nauseous that the government and these two churches as our caretakers because, in their view, we were savages unable to care for ourselves.

Years later Antone and Esther met and fell in love. They were married in Wisconsin, most likely in an Oneida Indian marriage ceremony. Elizabeth "Betsey" Hill was born to them on January 25, 1850, on the Oneida Indian Reservation in Wisconsin. Like her parents, Elizabeth had not been given the name Elizabeth at birth but had been given an Oneida Indian name: Aliskwat (Oneida for "Elizabeth"). Her parents called her this, as they only spoke the Oneida language, and Elizabeth called her parents the Oneida words for "Mom" and "Dad." Antone and Esther called each other by their Oneida names too. Before the US government forbade Oneida names—and all Oneida culture—Antone and Esther were able to pass along their Oneida heritage, including their language to Elizabeth. I am so grateful they were able to do this because it allowed Elizabeth to pass the culture and language along to her children too.

Elizabeth was an only child and tiny. According to my grandma Millie, Elizabeth loved to walk everywhere, and she commonly walked three to six miles a day as she got older. I was thrilled to learn this, as I am a runner and can easily run eight miles every other day. Elizabeth loved to smoke a homemade corncob pipe. Her home on the Oneida Reservation was a log cabin built most likely by Antone and other Oneidas. Because her family was poor, the house was very small and probably had one or two rooms. The family lived off of whatever crops they could grow, supplemented by government rations, fishing, and hunting to make ends meet. Grandma Millie told me that the Oneidas received flour and lard from the government, as did other tribes in the United States. The Navajo Indians used the flour and lard to make fry bread, which they invented in the 1860s after they were forced to walk three hundred miles from their ancestral lands in Arizona to resettle in New Mexico on lands that were unsuitable for growing vegetables and beans. The Navajos passed this recipe on to the Oneidas and to other Indian tribes.[7]

Elizabeth was feisty and full of life and proud to be Oneida Indian. She was true to her Native American heritage. She was proud of who she was. When I first learned I was half Oneida, a Native American tribe of the Iroquois Nation, *Oneida* was just a strange word to me. I didn't understand anything about being Oneida, and I was ashamed and not proud to be Indian like Elizabeth was. How could I be true to my Native American heritage when I knew nothing about it. I was actually prejudiced against my Indian heritage. I was prejudiced against myself!

Elizabeth was sixteen years old when she met an Oneida man named Nicholas Huff, and they married on December 2, 1866, in Oneida, Wisconsin. However, the US government did not accept this marriage as legal. *What? Why?* I wondered. I talked to elder Oneidas to find the answer. They told me that Elizabeth and Nicholas were married by an Oneida Indian traditional marriage ceremony. This meant that an Oneida chief or clan woman married them, or they followed other traditional marriage conventions.[8] Because the US government was trying to assimilate all Native America Indians in this country into the white European-derived culture, all Native American Indian customs, including traditional Indian marriage ceremonies like the one Elizabeth and Nicholas had, were forbidden. Thus, the government didn't recognize their marriage and didn't consider it legal. Only Christian marriages in a church were allowed and considered legal. I was really outraged to learn about this. Because their marriage was performed in Oneida Indian custom, the US government wouldn't even allow Nicholas and Elizabeth to live together in the same house.

Despite this, Elizabeth and Nicholas stayed in Oneida and had ten children together. Thank God, or I wouldn't be here today telling you this story! Grandma Millie also told me that Nicholas and Elizabeth never married, although I don't know if she actually believed this. I guess that if the US government forbade Oneida Indian marriage ceremonies, it would have been taboo to acknowledge that one had taken place. Back then, even showing your Indian culture and using your language meant big trouble from the government, so Grandma Millie may have feared repercussions for even mentioning the truth about this Oneida marriage. My Uncle Richard and other Oneida elders also told me that back then, and even today, Oneida feared such retribution. I believe that Elizabeth and Nicholas really were married.

US Census records indicate that Elizabeth and Nicholas lived near each other, and their ten children lived with Nicholas and all took his last name, Huff. I know that Elizabeth and Nicholas loved each other. The records from Oneida also listed Elizabeth as living with Martin McCormick in 1935, when actually, Elizabeth lived on Martin McCormick's land and not with Martin. This land was right near Nicholas Huff and their children's home. It's a shame that the US government did not recognize the Oneida marriage or let Nicholas and Elizabeth live together. I hated that the government discriminated against Elizabeth and Nicholas in this way.

All ten Huff children were given Oneida Indian names. The eldest, a son given the English name Henry, was given the Oneida name Ganyo. Since Oneida language is very difficult to speak I can't give a correct pronunciation of Ganyo. All of the children were raised in traditional Oneida culture and taught the Oneida language. Both parents took care of these ten children well. Their upbringing in Oneida traditions included teachings to be respectful of others, especially elders. Respect for elders was especially important in this culture, as the elderly were revered for their wisdom. This was especially so for elderly women, as the Oneida were very matriarchal.

Both the boys and girls did chores around the log house. The boys hunted and fished; the girls learned how to cook Oneida foods and sew clothes by hand. The children all wore moccasins and other clothing typical of Oneidas in that time period. Elizabeth made all of their clothes until the girls were old enough to help sew clothes themselves, including underwear out of flour-sack material. The Oneida did not wear buckskin loincloths or buckskin dresses, feathers in their hair, or war paint on their faces as I expected from the clothing on Indians on television.

I was also surprised that Oneida children were not hit for misbehavior. When I was naughty as a child, I was spanked, hit, made to kneel in a corner, and even made to eat Dial or Ivory soap as punishment. Instead, Elizabeth, Nicholas, and elders talked to their children to discipline them and to teach them life lessons through stories. I was never told stories that gave me life lessons. As I have come to learn, my siblings and I were not reprimanded by our parents or older relatives as our ancestors Elizabeth and Nicholas reprimanded their children. We were disciplined instead in the white Euro-American culture. I was absolutely shocked at the difference. I also learned that Oneidas had no swear words or slang. If you talk to any elder Native American Indian in this country from any tribe you will learn that there are no swear words in any Indians' languages. Check out the website, www. nativeamericannetroots/diary.1223, (2012) by Ojibwa. I swore when I was little and made to chew on soap because of it. Occasionally I swear as an adult today. Because swearing wasn't a part of my Oneida culture, I learned to swear from the white Euro-American culture I was raised in.

In 1874, my great-aunt Lily Huff was born, and my great-grandmother Sophia Josephine Huff was born two years later, on November 26, 1876.

There were some schools on the Oneida Reservation during this time. However, Elizabeth did not allow any of her children to attend school because the children were not allowed to speak Oneida there. I don't blame her. I know she would've allowed her children to attend school if they were allowed to speak their Oneida language and learn English. It was discriminatory of the US government to forbid Indian children all over America from speaking their native tongues. If Jews, Italians, Mexicans, African Americans, Spanish, Swedish, Germans, and people of other nationalities were forbidden to speak their native languages and forbidden to practice their native cultures, then who would these people be? They couldn't be themselves. This happened to Native American tribes throughout this country. We were forbidden to be Indian even though that is who we were! I can truly understand why Elizabeth didn't let her children attend school. She didn't want her kids to be assimilated into white culture when they were Oneida. Yes, she would've accepted her kids learning English, but she also wanted her kids to be raised Oneida as they were intended. This US government's assimilation plan was racist, and it really disturbs me, as I am sure it did Elizabeth, Nicholas, and many other Native American Indians here in this country. With our Indian cultures and languages forbidden, I ask again, who are we?

Between the 1870s and 1890s, the US government wanted to do something about what it called "the Indian problem." I was shocked to learn that all Indians here in America were a problem to the US government! Why were Native American Indians a problem to the US government while people of other nationalities were not a problem? I found that it cost the US government more to kill an Indian in this country through warfare than to assimilate an Indian into white culture through education![9] Wow, killing one of us Indians was expensive! I have to admit I was surprised that Indians were just a financial consideration for the government. African Americans were used as slaves by the white Americans, so they had been considered problems too. Hmm … since Indians owned their own lands, they were a problem. And since it was cheaper to assimilate Indians into white culture, the US government decided to do so. I was appalled that the US government did not accept my Oneida ancestors' culture, language, and heritage, and I was floored that it was considered better for all Indians in our country to be assimilated into white culture than to let Indians be themselves. I can't believe my ancestors were considered savages who needed to be saved and lifted up into Christianity!

As the US government put its assimilation plan in motion, it even went so far as to forcefully remove many Indian children from their homes and parents and sent them to faraway boarding schools. This was done to assimilate these children into the white culture by forcing them to live in faraway communities among white Americans. Keeping them from returning to their reservations freed up even more land for white settlers to move onto and reduced the government financial burden of supporting the Indians living on reservations. The government also hoped that Indians would breed with non-Indians, thus further diluting Native American heritage and providing more land for whites and non-Indians. In the end, the assimilation plan was all about the land.

The government assigned agents to all reservations in America to enforce their policy of subjugation over the Indians forced to live there. The agents were usually non-Indian. Besides overseeing and governing over the reservation lands, these agents were responsible for the Indians' name changes, for they had the power to refuse to record the people's Indian names. This was done not only to keep track of Indian families living on the reservations but also to assimilate the Indians.

For Elizabeth, Nicholas, and the rest of the Oneidas, life on the reservation wasn't easy. The Oneida Reservation was isolated and much smaller than promised. Grandma Millie told me things were pretty bleak. Unemployment was high, and the US agents overseeing the reservation had complete control of everything. Oneidas were told to learn English and speak only English, as all tribes across America were. When Elizabeth was told to do this, it did not sit well with her. I don't blame her for not wanting to give up her language and her Oneida self. And she didn't! She absolutely refused to change into someone she was not. She was Indian and wanted to stay Indian, and she kept her children from attending the school that forbade the Oneida language.

That Elizabeth and her children were required to stop being Indian brings me to tears. It broke my heart to learn about this part of my background, and it breaks my heart that my Oneida heritage and language couldn't be passed on down to me.

The US government punished Elizabeth and Nicholas by removing their children from home. I do not know how many of the children were taken away, nor do I know where they were all placed, but I do know that two of the children— Sophia Josephine Huff, my great-grandmother, and her sister Lily Huff, my great-aunt—were sent far away to a boarding school, Carlisle Indian Industrial Boarding School located in Carlisle. Pennsylvania, in July of 1891. Although her children were taken away, Elizabeth's spirit was not broken. She kept her Oneida tongue and culture. She kept her dignity and never, ever lost her love for the children who were taken away from her. I admire her strength and resolve. She was Oneida Indian and stayed true to her roots. It would be years before she would see her relocated children, but her love for them sustained her.

Sophia Josephine Huff-Powless, 1960s

I met my great-grandmother Sophia Huff in the early 1960s, when I was a child living on the South Side of Milwaukee, Wisconsin. She was in her late eighties at that time, and I was around seven or eight years old. Grandma Millie had brought Great-Grandma Sophie (as we called her) over to my house on South Thirty-sixth Street and Greenfield Avenue. Great-Grandma Sophie was very short and very petite—maybe four feet ten and ninety pounds soaking wet. She wore dark clothing, and she wore her hair, which was white in the front and black in the back, up in a bun. She was quiet but very kind to my siblings and me. Before I met her that day, I hadn't even known about her. It was as if she came out of the woodwork. It really bothered me that I had never met her before.

My family was having some sort of celebration the day that Great-Grandma Sophie was introduced to us. As the adults started to prepare food for this get together, Sophie jumped right in to help. She worked tirelessly and seemed to have a ton of energy. I was shy then and afraid to get to know her or even talk to her that day. I didn't know what to say.

I studied her bun. She seemed to have a lot of hair. Then when I saw her undo her hair for bed, I discovered that she had the longest hair! Grandma Millie said that Sophie never cut her hair. She braided it and then coiled it into a bun on the top of her head daily. I later learned that it was tradition for Oneida women to wear their hair long and to only cut it when they were in mourning. Because her hair was so long, she took her time to comb out her hair by herself. Usually she sat down to comb it, and because she was so short, her hair seemed to be as long as she was tall! I would've loved to have helped her comb out her hair, but I was just a kid. I watched from the hallway with my brother Butch as he and I stood there watching her unbraid and comb her hair.

I learned that Sophia lived with Grandma Millie and other relatives in Milwaukee during this time. Many of my relatives lived in Milwaukee to earn a living. I thought that all my relatives had always lived in Milwaukee. Most of them were actually born in Oneida, Wisconsin, on the Oneida Indian Reservation. But my relatives could find no work on the reservation, so they moved Milwaukee, Chicago, and other big cities to find jobs. When I met her, Sophia still worked as a cleaning lady for white ladies in the Milwaukee area although she was well into her eighties, and she never retired. Grandma Millie told me Sophia never had to work out like we do today to keep her figure tiny because she worked all the time. When she visited us, whether it for a holiday or a birthday, she always pitched in and helped out. Her work ethic and willingness to help impressed me.

She never called us kids by our names, but there were now ten of us, so it was hard for some relatives to remember who was who. When she wanted help from one of us or wanted to teach us how to do something, she would say, "Hey, kid, come here." Even though she was reserved, she was a feisty woman, fair and honest. Even as a kid I was surprised at her endless energy. She could do a lot of things: she could cook from scratch and was an excellent cook, Grandma Millie told me, and she could garden and sew, to name a few.

Once she showed my older brother Butch how to make a braided rug from strips of rags. She called this a rag rug. I had never heard of anything like this before. She had learned to make these from her mother, Elizabeth, in Oneida. It amazed me that a rug could be made out of rags. Oneida Indians made these rag rugs for the wood or dirt floors of their log homes.

I noticed that she seemed to really like music a lot, and her favorite television show was *The Lawrence Welk Show*, a musical variety show that aired on Saturday nights in Milwaukee. She moved her chair close to the television so she could see and hear everything and remained glued to the tube throughout the show.

One New Year's Eve my sister Renee and I stayed overnight at Grandma Millie's apartment to keep Great-Grandma Sophie company while Grandma Millie went out to celebrate. The three of us went to bed around 9:00 p.m. Great-Grandma Sophie slept in one room and my sister Renee and I slept in the other. In the middle of the night Renee and I were awakened by a banging on our bedroom door. It was Great-Grandma Sophie. She yelled, "*Hoyan, hoyan!*" I didn't know what that meant. She continued yelling, "Hoyan!" and giggled as she handed Renee a new pair of gloves and me a scarf as presents. Then she left the room, closed our bedroom door, and went back to her room giggling.

Years later I learned that *hoyan* meant "happy New Year" in the Oneida language. Hoyan was an Oneida tradition in which Oneida children on the reservation traveled from home to home on the morning of New Year's Day yelling, "Hoyan, hoyan!"[10] At each house, residents gave the children treats of homemade donuts, fruit, or candy. I never celebrated this holiday when I was growing up, but I would have loved to have participated in this celebration myself and to have taken my own sons outside to visit other neighbors to celebrate. I even would have loved to have baked donuts to give out to my own children and neighborhood kids.

Renee wore those gloves out she loved them so much, and I wore my scarf as long as I could. Great-Grandma Sophie was so kind to give us these gifts and to introduce us to Hoyan. Renee and I still cherish this memory today.

Another time in the early 1960s, Great-Grandma Sophie came over to our home for Easter dinner. I remember her sitting at a table in our dining room peeling potatoes for dinner. As she sat peeling away, my younger sister Sherry peeked into the dining room to watch Sophia working. Sophia looked up at Sherry and spoke a strange language to her. The rest of us kids just sat nearby and listened to her speak. We didn't know what she was saying, as we had never heard this language before. This scared Sherry, and she ran into the kitchen to hide, and Great-Grandma Sophie just giggled and giggled. Two more times Sherry peeked into the dining room at Sophia, and each time Sophia saw her and spoke the same strange language to Sherry, Sherry ran away to the small kitchen, and Sophia giggled hysterically. Still none of us kids knew what Sophia was saying.

Years later we found out she had been speaking the Oneida language. We kids only knew English. How could Sophia be bilingual in the Oneida language and English, and why didn't my siblings and I know the Oneida language when we were half Oneida?

I am grateful that I got to meet and get to know a little about Great-Grandma Sophie, including her sense of humor from this Easter visit. She didn't come over to visit us a lot, but I enjoyed it when she did visit, and we all loved her and respected her. I realize now that Sophia didn't visit us ten kids more because she worked often to clean homes to make ends meet. In my heart I wanted to get to know her better. Oh my, the things I could've learned about being Oneida from her! My research into her life has helped me to get to know her and my Oneida culture better.

From the 1960s to the 1990s, Grandma Millie often mentioned that Sophia had attended a school in Carlisle, Pennsylvania, and bragged that a man named Jim Thorpe had been her classmate. Initially, I didn't know who Jim Thorpe was, as I was quite young, but then as a child I saw a movie on our black-and-white television called *Jim Thorpe: All American*. Though this movie was originally made in 1951, I first saw it in the '60s, and it played on television a lot. The main character was a man with really dark hair and dark skin named Jim Thorpe who was a terrific athlete at a school named Carlisle. This man, Jim Thorpe was a Sac and Fox Indian and a great football player. When I heard the name Carlisle mentioned in the movie, I immediately made the connection with Great-Grandma Sophie. Since Sophia and this great athlete on television both went to Carlisle, the school seemed prestigious to me. It must have been a special school for smart, athletic, talented students to go to. I was just mesmerized as I watched this movie on television and was in awe of Jim Thorpe and of Carlisle!

Later, I often wondered why Sophia had gone to this school with Jim Thorpe. Why had she attended a school so far away from Wisconsin and her family? No one in the family ever said why. Nobody ever said that this school's full name was Carlisle Indian Industrial Boarding School. I didn't know what an industrial school for Indians was. I didn't understand the purpose of having an industrial boarding school for Indians. No one said this school was just for Native American children. Relatives only mentioned that Sophia attended Carlisle with Jim Thorpe.

After seeing this movie on television, I honestly thought that the actor portraying Jim Thorpe, Burt Lancaster, was actually Jim Thorpe. Being young, it didn't register in my brain that Thorpe's character was played by a white actor with dyed black hair and skin darkened with makeup to look like a Sac and Fox Indian. I also didn't know where Carlisle was, other than it was located on the East Coast of the United States. However, because I associated Carlisle with this great athlete Jim Thorpe, I also bragged that my great-grandma Sophie went to this school with this famous man! My thinking that Burt Lancaster was Jim Thorpe is understandable now since I also did not know I was looking at an American Indian when I looked at myself in the mirror each day.

I have since learned that Sophia was not a classmate of Jim Thorpe's and that Carlisle was not a special school like Harvard or Yale. Sophia attended Carlisle only one year, from 1891 until 1892, and Jim Thorpe attended Carlisle years later, long after Sophia had left. I was very surprised to learn this, as I had always thought that Sophia and Jim were classmates! Jim Thorpe attended Carlisle for one year, 1904 through 1905. He then returned to Carlisle in 1907 and stayed until 1909. He returned to Carlisle again in 1911 and stayed through 1912, putting Carlisle on the map because of his great athletic skills in football, track and other sports. His performance in the 1912 Olympics is well documented. Jim Thorpe left Carlisle for good in 1912, but contrary to historical articles and media reports, Jim Thorpe did not graduate from Carlisle.

Carlisle Indian Industrial Boarding School was never a college, as reported.[11] Instead, from 1879 to 1918, it was an experimental school set up by the US government to assimilate Native American children from across the United States into the white American society. This first school of its kind got its name from its location in the town of Carlisle, Pennsylvania, on an abandoned army base. The *Industrial* part of its name came from its purpose to prepare Indian children from across the country to become servants or do menial labor as they learned English and white customs. It was called a boarding school because the children lived in dorms on the gated campus. So, Sophia did not sit next to Jim Thorpe in the second grade at Carlisle because she didn't attend the second grade. She wasn't put in any grade because she couldn't speak English when she first arrived at Carlisle. She sat in a classroom half of each day to learn English. Because she wasn't in attendance at the same time as Thorpe, Jim did not wave at her in classroom as my relatives had mentioned. My relatives fabricated this story to sugar coat Carlisle's image as an educational school, not an assimilation experiment. Another relative told me that her mother, whose name I will not mention out of respect for my relative's privacy, did go to school with Jim Thorpe, but this is also not true. Her mother attended Carlisle from 1916 to 1918, when the school officially closed. Jim Thorpe was already long gone from Carlisle and playing professional baseball and football in major US cities. I can understand why my relatives glorified this school's connection to Jim Thorpe: doing so sugarcoated Carlisle's true purpose, making it easier for my older relatives to not have to explain to us younger generations that the school had really been set up to assimilate Indians into white culture.

Not only did I not know anything about Native Americans into adulthood, but my Oneida heritage was not discussed much. The only Indians I knew were the ones I saw on television in Western movies, sitcoms, and even commercials portrayed as savages, villains, and vicious killers. The Indians took scalps of non-Indians, screamed unrecognizable words, and acted inhuman. I wasn't one of these Indians! I even rooted for the cowboys, cavalry, and non-Indian settlers when I watched TV because the Indians I saw were overbearing, overwhelming, and downright *bad*. But, in truth, Indians had actually been overwhelmed by whites or other non-Indians who wanted their lands. I disliked the Indians on television, who made loud whooping sounds and could only mutter words like *how* or *ugg!* They always wore war paint on their faces and feathers in their hair, and they lived in teepees. They were dirty, wild, and crazy and seemed to kill non-Indians for no reason. In honesty, those television Indians were *stereotypes* created by Hollywood, and I believed that Indians here in this country were really like that. No wonder I always rooted for the non-Indian people.

I never did see a realistic Native American image when I was growing up. Of course, I also didn't know that the Indian tribes in America were native, or indigenous, to this country. Today, I am shocked by the fact that Native American Indians were portrayed so inaccurately on television. I am also shocked that I was not taught about my Oneida Indian heritage or language. My husband, Charles, is 100 percent Italian, and he knows a lot about his Italian culture, including Italian cooking and customs, and even some of the language. He knows who he is. I, on the other hand, didn't know who I was for a long time.

I saw another Western movie on television in the '60s called *Cheyenne Autumn*. This movie, made in 1964 and starring the Richard Widmark, also falsely portrayed Indians. In one scene Richard Widmark, dressed in a cavalry soldier's uniform, says to an actress, "It takes a blue coat to make a white man a soldier, but a Cheyenne is a soldier from the first slap on his bottom." Talk about labeling an Indian just out of the womb on his birthday! This exact quote is listed in the original script of Cheyenne Autumn, available at www.quotes.net/movies/2056

A commercial that aired in the '70s shows an actor named Iron Eyes Cody crying because of how polluted America had become. He is dressed in buckskin clothing and a big feathered headdress. As he cries, he says, "People start pollution, and people can stop it." He looked Indian to me based on the stereotypes I knew, and I thought Iron Eyes Cody was a real Native American. Boy, was I wrong! Iron Eyes Cody was 100 percent second-generation Sicilian named Espera Oscar de Corti!

Over the years, I saw many other actors who were not Indian portray Indians, including Anthony Quinn, Burt Lancaster, Burt Reynolds, Chuck Conners, Boris Karloff (who should have stuck to horror films), Sylvester Stallone (who should stick with Rocky or Rambo), Charles Bronson, and William Shatner (who should with *Star Trek*). I learned that Hollywood usually did not want real Indians to portray Indians on television or movies. Then *Dances with Wolves* came out in 1990 and was one of the first movies I could remember seeing in which real Indians portrayed Indians! Though this movie centered on a white cavalry soldier portrayed by Kevin Costner, I was glad to see real Indians acting as Indians, and I was pleased that they were portrayed as real humans with feelings and not as wild, crazy, inhuman savages like those I had seen on TV when I was growing up.

When I was in the fourth grade, a boy in my class called me a "Jap," and he sneered as he said it. I wondered why he called me this and why he looked down on me as he said it, as if I were awful and dirty. At that time I didn't know what a Jap was, but I later learned that this was a derogatory term for Japanese people and that Japanese here in America were actually imprisoned in camps here in our own country during World War II. Many of them were U.S. Citizens! The US government interned them in prison camps for fear that some of them could be spies for Japan. I felt sad for these Japanese who were discriminated against and mistreated here in America by our own government just because our country was at war with Japan.[12] Learning about the Japanese being treated like this made me nauseous, and I didn't like that boy in my fourth grade class looking down on me and meanly calling me Jap. When this boy treated me so rudely, I didn't really know what nationality I was, although I had also been mistaken as being part Chinese, Mexican, and other nationalities. I knew it just wasn't right for someone to talk down to someone else or to be rude, no matter what nationality the other person was.

Years later I found out that my relatives and elders didn't feel comfortable discussing our Oneida Indian heritage with my siblings and me. It had been taboo for them to share their Native American culture with their children. In the past to practice your Oneida culture brought painful repercussions from the government. I think that fear haunted them long after they left the reservation. Perhaps this fear stemmed from a kind of post-traumatic stress syndrome. As a result, many Native American Indians, including me, never did get the opportunity to learn of our heritage and language. Today many Native American Indians are trying to learn their cultures and languages, and I am one of them. Thank God, our Creator that we are, so we can pass this knowledge along to our children and future generations without fear!

Sophia Huff: Her Early Years, November 1876 to September 1892

ince Sophia was born on November 25, 1876, more than 139 years ago, I have had to ask family members and elder relatives about her. When she was born on the Oneida Indian Reservation, her parents gave her an Oneida name. Unfortunately, when her Indian name was changed to the English name Sophia, a record was not kept of her Oneida name. I searched and searched to try to find out her Oneida name, but sadly, I've not been able to do so. Sophia's mother, Elizabeth, would never have changed her daughter's Oneida name to Sophia, so I have no doubt that Sophia was given this name by US agents on the Oneida Reservation or by census workers assigned to oversee the reservation in the late 1800s. Changing Oneida names to English names was commonplace on all reservations. This was part of the government's assimilation process. I learned from Grandma Millie that Sophia did not like to be called "Sophia" and preferred "Sofia," so most people called her that. She pronounced her name "SO-phy-ya", so most people called her that, using her pronunciation. When I first met her in the early 1960's, she was introduced to my nine siblings and me as great-grandma Sophie. She was one of ten children born to Elizabeth and Nicholas. Like her mother, she was very tiny, but people told me that her feistiness made up for her small stature. She was baptized Episcopal at the Holy Apostles Episcopal Church in Oneida, Wisconsin, on January 7, 1877. Her sponsors were Baptist Doxtator, Jerusha Skenandore, and Margaret Baird.

My great-aunt Lily had been born in 1874 and baptized Episcopal on September 28, 1877. Lily's sponsors were her parents and the church's Reverend Frances A. Goodenough. Lily had also been given an Oneida Indian name and received her English from a US agent or census worker. The US government was very keen on assimilating all Native Americans across the country to white culture, and part of the assimilation process was to change their names to English names. To this day I am outraged that my ancestors were forced to change their names to appease the US government.[13]

Despite the assimilation process going on about them, Elizabeth and Nicholas raised their children as Oneida Indians, just as they had been raised. Though very poor, the children took care of the log house they lived in, did their chores, and learned about the Oneida culture and language. As I mentioned earlier, Elizabeth and Nicholas did not allow Sophia and her siblings to attend school in the area because their Oneida language was forbidden there and only English allowed.

Like her mother, Esther, had, Elizabeth sewed all of her children's clothing. These were typical garments for Oneidas at this time, such as broadcloth or simple cotton dresses, loose blouses, and skirts wrapped about the waist for girls and cotton pants and shirts for the boys. Everyone wore moccasins. Everyone wore their hair long, as Oneida men and women never cut their hair unless they were in mourning. This was different from my experience, as Grandma Millie cut my sisters' and my hair really short, into pixie cuts, and I wore that style for a long time.

Sophia had a beautiful singing voice, according to Grandma Millie, who heard her sing around the house as she was doing housework. Grandma Millie quietly listened to her mother sing. When Grandma

Millie was 102, she told me that if there was one thing that she could still do, it would have been to sing as well as her mother! She tried to sing like Sophia, but she knew her voice wasn't like her mother's.

I was surprised to learn that Sophia didn't live in a teepee, as Indians on television did, but in what was called a longhouse when her family lived in New York and then in a log home after they were forced to relocate to Wisconsin. The family's situation was worsening when Sophia was born. To make ends meet, relatives banded together to live. Beginning in 1849, the US government allowed white settlers to move onto Oneida lands, as Wisconsin had become a state. Non-Indian loggers cut down a lot of timber, and with the loss of woods, animals moved elsewhere for shelter and food. The loss of animals limited the hunting for the Oneidas. During this time much of the land left to the Oneidas was even smaller. Farms on the reservation were small and used to grow crops for the Oneidas to sustain themselves. Jobs were scarce on the reservation, and Oneidas couldn't find jobs off the reservation because they were Indians! The log house that Sophia and her siblings were raised in no longer stands, but the reservation features some replica log houses on display for visitors to see. When I drove Grandma Millie over to see these replicas, she remembered seeing these types of homes in Oneida when she was a little girl in the early 1900s.

I wasn't able to see the Oneida Reservation until I was an adult, so I asked Grandma Millie what life had been like there way back when. She said the reservation was poor in general. It had no electricity, so people used candles or pig rind for lighting. It also had no indoor plumbing, so if someone had to go to the bathroom, that person had to use the outhouse behind the house—outdoors! Grandma Millie explained that when the outhouse hole was full, the men would dig a new hole nearby, lift up the outhouse, and move it over the newly dug hole. Then, "That old shit-filled hole was covered up with dirt!" Grandma Millie said. Sophia and her family collected water from nearby Duck Creek or collected rainwater in wooden barrels set near the log house. This water was used for laundry, which was washed by hand using a scrub board. Sponge baths were the norm because people had no indoor tubs or showers like we have today. Woodstoves heated the log homes, and everyone in the family took turns collecting wood for the stove.

Being poor, many on the reservation did not own a car. Instead, most people walked everywhere, but some rode a horse if they had one or rode in a horse-drawn wagon or sleigh in the winter with neighbors. Grandma Millie said most Oneidas lived in run-down log homes that really looked like shacks. She said conditions were bleak when she lived on the reservation as a child. Oneida Indians did their best to survive under these very poor conditions.

Grandma Millie and other elders told me that social events centered on the local churches. Sophia and her family went go to functions such as picnics, bake sales, pie-eating contests, church services, and gatherings for basket weaving, lace making, quilt making, Oneida singing, and corn husking held at the Holy Apostles Episcopal Church. I was surprised that Sophia was Episcopal and that some of my other late relatives were also Catholic and Methodist. What I had seen on TV had led me to believe that Indians didn't have any religion.

Sophia lived on the Oneida Indian Reservation from her birth on November 25, 1876, to July 1891, when she and her older sister Lily were forcefully taken away from their parents and sent by train to the Carlisle Indian Industrial Boarding School hundreds of miles away in Pennsylvania, just as Indian children from all over the country were being forced from their homes and reservations to attend faraway boarding schools. This was done to punish their mother, Elizabeth, for her refusal to stop being Oneida Indian and assimilate into white culture. I am and was appalled to learn that the US government did this. This was outrageous! I resent the US government for forcing my Oneida ancestors to lose their Oneida culture, language, and identity. How would the US government like it if the shoe were on the other foot and its members were forbidden to speak English, dress in European-style clothes, eat European-style foods, or even live in European-style homes?

In July of 1891 Mrs. Mary Campbell, then a teacher at Carlisle, traveled by train with her husband and two former Oneida Indian students to Oneida to scout prospective students. The two former Oneida students spoke fluent Oneida and English, so these two young men served as interpreters between the children, none of whom could speak English, and the Campbell's. In the end, twenty-six Oneida children—twelve boys and fourteen girls, two of whom were Sophia and Lily—accompanied the Campbell's and the two former Oneida student recruiters on a train from Oneida, Wisconsin, to Carlisle, Pennsylvania. The trip took about three days, as Carlisle was 650 miles away from Oneida, with a stop to switch trains in Chicago.

The June 12, 1891, issue of the *Indian Helper*, a newspaper printed by the Carlisle Indian Industrial Boarding School at that time, mentioned:

> Mr. and Mrs. Campbell traveling by train to Montana and Wisconsin to visit two Indian Agencies. They will bring back a party of pupils if they run across any who are anxious to come to the Carlisle Indian Boarding School. But, Carlisle Indian Industrial Boarding School has arrived at a stage of progress where applicants brought back must be of excellent material, both in health and scholarship to gain admission.

I cringe when I read that applicants had to gain admission to Carlisle Boarding School when, in reality, most Indian children were forced to attend. I'm sure Sophia, Lily, and the twenty-four other children were very smart and healthy, but I know that Sophia and Lily were not anxious to come to Carlisle. They were forced to go there, as most children who attended were. Thus, the *Indian Helper* is not telling the truth. Carlisle was the first boarding school created for Indian children in this country. It was created as an experiment for assimilating these children into white culture. Sophia and Lily's attendance at Carlisle was mandated by the US government by the year 1891.[14]

Elizabeth, Nicholas, and the parents of other twenty-six children sent to Carlisle were devastated to have their children forcefully taken from them and sent far away. I know this in my heart, for if my two children were taken away from my husband and I and sent to a faraway school, we would've been heartbroken and very upset at the US government for taking our kids away to become non-Indian and more "civilized."

The government misled parents by saying the children would be taught to be better citizens if sent to a boarding school. But Sophia and Lily didn't have to be sent away from their parents to become assimilated to become better American citizens. Oneidas and all other Native Americans were the original citizens of the country called the United States of America. Not only did I not know that I was Oneida Indian as a child, but I also didn't know that my family was a native to this country.

When Sophia attended Carlisle, her citizenship training entailed removing anything in her behavior that was Oneida Indian. Half of each weekday was spent learning English. The rest of her days consisted of lessons in domestic or other menial jobs because the US government had decided that Native American Indians were not very smart intellectually and thus could only handle subservient jobs. I find this repulsive.

So, in late June 1891, the Campbell's and two Oneida student recruiters came with Oneida Reservation agents to Nicholas and Elizabeth's home to forcefully remove Sophia and Lily. Sadly, Nicholas and Elizabeth had no say in this matter. They objected to the two girls being taken away, but the threat of punishment by the US agents assigned to the reservation prevented them from being able to take any action to keep their children home.

This was a very traumatic day for Elizabeth and Nicholas. I know Sophia and Lily went with the Campbell's, recruiters, and agents willingly to spare their parents any punishment, which could have been anything, including being locked up behind bars, being beaten, having rations taken away, or even being killed by the agents who ran the reservation.

Sophia and Lily boarded the train with the twenty-four other Oneida children for the long trip east to Carlisle, Pennsylvania. None of these kids had ever been away from home. None of these kids had ever been on a train. It must have been so strange to board this huge metal machine that moved for Sophia and the other children, and they were very scared. Sophia was only fourteen and Lily sixteen. They hugged each other, and all the children huddled together for comfort. The Campbells had the two Oneida student recruiters translate to the children that they would be able to return home for summers and holidays. This was not true, but it pacified the children somewhat. All of the children sobbed uncontrollably. Their parents sobbed too, and their hearts ached. Sophia and Lily hoped that the non-Indian agents assigned to Oneida Reservation would not punish their parents further, but they did worry. All the children were upset and unsure why they had to go to school so far away from their homes. Of course, they had no clue that they were to be assimilated into the white culture at Carlisle.

As the train moved slowly away from the Oneida Depot, Sophia looked out the window and sobbed so hard she could barely see her parents on the platform, let alone the familiar Oneida lands she was leaving. All the children looked around inside the train and at each other, totally helpless. They looked at the two Oneida student recruiters' European-style clothing and short haircuts. Both of these young men spoke fluent English with the Campbells and would occasionally speak Oneida to the children, telling them, "You will become better people and better citizens, and you will learn much at Carlisle." These two men said this to reassure the children that things would be good for them.

After crying for a very long time, the children hugged each other, their noses sniffling, their shoulders heaving, and their bodies just plain old tired out from crying so hard and so long. They all grew quiet as the train chugged along toward the East Coast. Besides the Campbells and two Oneida student recruiters, everyone else on the train was non-Indian. Most of them spoke English. Soon the train climbed and descended hills, and the children peered out the windows to see mountainous countryside.

I don't know exactly how long the train ride from Wisconsin to Pennsylvania took; although I estimate that it took around three days. After all this time, the children could feel the train slow. They could hear the train chugging slower. The brakes squealed as the train drew to a complete stop. Another whistle blew loudly. All of a sudden, a white man in a strange hat motioned toward a door that opened onto the wooden platform. All of the children, the two student recruiters, and the Campbell's stepped onto the platform and were met by more white people. Sophia and the other children were scared. Sophia wondered, *Where in the world am I?* The children were led through very tall wooden gates and into Carlisle Indian Industrial Boarding School campus. Although I do not know what time of day Sophia, Lily, and the rest of the children arrived at Carlisle, they all arrived on July 8, 1891.

An article in *The Indian Helper* from July 10, 1891, says: "Mr. and Mrs. Campbell and two male Oneida student recruiters have arrived at Carlisle by train with twelve boys and fourteen girls from Oneida, Wisconsin."

These children's names were not mentioned in the article, as most of these children probably went by their Oneida names. The newspaper wasn't about to print any Indian names let alone any English names. I surmise that the names were excluded to prevent historians and relatives such as me from documenting just who these twenty-six kids were. Many records from the era when Richard H. Pratt served as superintendent of Carlisle from 1879 to 1904 are missing and were possibly destroyed. Luckily, documents at the National Archives and Records Administration (NARA) in Washington, DC, listed Sophia and Lily Huff as two of these twenty-six Oneida children.

All the children and recruiters were very tired from this long train trip as they were escorted through the school grounds. The grounds were completely surrounded by an approximately seven-foot-tall fence built by Carlisle students and Indians who were former prisoners of Fort Marion in Florida to keep the Indian students in and the white settlers out.[15] All of the children were led into a building, and then the twelve boys were directed into one room and Sophia, Lily, and the other girls were directed to a different room.

The other girls were then told to remove all of their clothing, moccasins, trinkets, necklaces, medicine bags, and any other Oneida artifacts. One girl did not want to remove her necklace, so a white matron took it off the girl's neck and threw it into the pile of Oneida items on the floor. This matron and other white matrons led the girls to a large shower room and motioned for each girl to get under the water spray. The matrons proceeded to scrub down each girl. Sophia wondered why she and the other girls had to be cleaned by these matrons. The girls were crying. After being scrubbed, the girls had a strange chemical rubbed into their hair, which Grandma Millie told me was to kill any head lice the girls may have had. The girls then stood in line naked and very cold.

Next the matrons handed the girls very heavy Victorian-style dresses, underwear, hard-toed shoes, slips, and stockings to put on and one by one the girls were told to put their hair up in buns or in braids behind their heads. One girl refused to do anything to her hair, and the matrons immediately cut her hair into a short pixie cut. Scared that her hair might get cut too, Sophia immediately put her braids up into a bun on top of her head as instructed. Her feet felt very uncomfortable in the hard-toed shoes, as she had only ever worn moccasins, and the heavy cloth of the dress was also very uncomfortable in the summer heat.

All of a sudden a few girls started wailing loudly. Sophia looked over at them to see what they were crying about when she noticed that there outside the window on the lawn, all the girls' clothes, trinkets, moccasins, and other Oneida artifacts were burning in a big fire. Sophia broke down crying too, not understanding why all her belongings were being burned. The white staffs, having done this for years now, were far removed from feeling for these children during this ordeal. The children were shocked, hurt, confused, and heartbroken to see their belongings burned. As the girls cried, the boys joined them and wailed too upon seeing the girls' European-style looks. All the boys had had their hair cut short or shaved and had been given uniforms to wear. Their belongings, too, were burned; however, my research indicated that some of the white staff—including Superintendent Pratt—kept some items as souvenirs. I was horrified to learn about the children's trauma.

After receiving their new clothes, shoes, and hairstyles, Sophia and the other children were directed to yet another room with a huge blackboard on the wall. Oh, Sophia's feet hurt so badly from the tight shoes! On this blackboard were strange words written in white. The children stared at the board. They had never seen a blackboard before, let alone the writing on it! The strange writing was English names written in chalk. Sophia and Lily were asked to move to sit in chairs at the back of the room, and the rest of the children were given a pointer and asked to point to an English name on the blackboard. These kids had no clue what these names were much less what they meant. As each kid pointed to a name, a staff member then wrote that name on paper and pinned it to the child's clothes. This name would be the child's name from now on. All of the children were forbidden to use their Indian names ever again at Carlisle. Since Sophia and Lily had already been given English names in Oneida, Wisconsin, they just watched this process. Sophia whispered Lily's Oneida name. One of the matrons overheard her say something in Oneida and immediately slapped Sophia's hands with a ruler. Sophia, Lily, and all the other children were shocked.

The children were confused by their new names. In their traditional culture, people had a variety of formal and informal names that reflected their relationships and life experiences. These names had had meaning for the children and their families. Thus, this renaming was extremely difficult for these kids. The children couldn't read the names and had picked them only by the way the writing looked on the blackboard, and these new English names had no meaning for these Indian children. That these children were renamed shocked me and has left me with a heavy heart. What was wrong with our Native American Indian names? What was so wrong with our culture that we had to be given new clothes, a new language, and a culture? Well, all the assimilation of Native Americans saved the US government money, allowed them to control those they considered inhuman savages, and allowed them to take our land and give it away to settlers of European heritage.

On the following page is a photo of Sophia and Lily taken in 1891, (fig. 2) when they first arrived at Carlisle Indian Industrial Boarding School. They look very Victorian in their new clothing and hairdos. Carlisle's school photographer, John N. Choate, had the girls pose with Sophia standing and Lily sitting on the chair beside her sister. This picture was taken to show everyone outside Carlisle Boarding School how much Carlisle had refined Sophia and Lily from unkempt, wild Indians to civilized humans. This picture was called the "after picture" because Sophia and Lily were no longer dressed as Indians but dressed as whites. This picture was probably labeled as the after picture by Carlisle Photographer John N. Coate or Carlisle staff. I haven't been able to find a "before" picture taken of Sophia and Lily in their Oneida clothing and hairstyles, but Carlisle did take before pictures of other children when they first arrived. Carlisle used these pictures as propaganda to show the world how these children had been changed to fit into Euro-American white culture. Some of these photos were sold as postcards for profit! [16]

Figure 2-Sophia and Lily Huff, dressed in their Carlisle
clothing, July, 1891. Courtesy Cumberland County
Historical Society. John N. Choate-photographer.

Sophia, Lily, and the other girls were led to the porch off the girls' dormitory. This is where they would sleep. The dormitory was having an addition put in July 1891, so there wasn't enough room for all the new students. Lily was immediately separated from Sophia. In fact, all the Oneida girls were placed with girls from other tribes. The dormitory had canvass covering the top of the porch to protect the girls from the elements outdoors. Later on Sophia was moved into a new dorm room with two other Indian girls from two different tribes, ensuring they wouldn't speak their tribal languages. I don't know how the girls communicated, but I'd guess that they used a lot of sign language and other nonverbal cues to converse. Anyone caught speaking their native tongue were immediately punished.

Sophia and Lily never saw each other again. Carlisle had plans for Lily!

Figure 3-John N. Choate photo, courtesy Cumberland County Historical Society. This dormitory is where Sophia lived for one year, from July, 1891 until September, 1892.

A few days after arriving at Carlisle, Lily and a group of girls from other tribes were summoned to a big room and told to stand up tall in a straight line. A few minutes later, a group of white Quaker ladies and other white settler ladies from Pennsylvania, New Jersey, Maryland, Delaware, New York, and other parts of the East Coast entered the room. In turn, each white woman walked up and down the line of girls, looking each girl over and then selecting one to live with her as her servant. A Quaker lady chose Lily to live with her in the New Jersey countryside. Lily was shocked. She thought she was coming to Carlisle Indian Industrial Boarding School to become a better citizen, learn English, and get an education, and she had arrived at Carlisle maybe three days before. Lily never returned to Carlisle. She spent years working as a servant for various white families on the East Coast.

The Quaker family paid Lily for her work, and she was allowed to keep half of her earnings.[17] The other half was sent back to Carlisle and put into an account for safe keeping. So, instead of becoming a student at Carlisle, Lily had been put into the school's Outing Program, which placed Carlisle Indian students with white families away from the school to work as servants or in other menial jobs. Lily was surprised and very afraid. She could not speak English at all and really hadn't gone to Carlisle to learn anything after all, showing that the *Indian Helper*'s comment that "Carlisle was making progress, thus wanted students who were of excellent material and scholarship to enter the school" wasn't the truth. Lily's parents also thought that Carlisle intended to educate Lily to become a better citizen and had no clue that Lily was sent away to be a servant to a white family.

I found it interesting; therefore, that Lily was listed as a student at Carlisle although she never really was a student there. The US government paid Carlisle a certain amount of money per student, and because Lily was listed as a student there, Carlisle received money for Lily's schooling even when she didn't attend, and half of Lily's earnings as a servant were sent back to Carlisle. I don't know whether Lily eventually received saved earnings from Carlisle, but I do know that some students in her position did not receive their earnings from the school. Carlisle kept the money if students bolted from their outings to return to the tribe or were insubordinate, and used some of the students' money as collateral for building projects such as the gymnasium. According to records from NARA, Lily attended more than one outing. According to the school's rules, a student had to sign an agreement to go to an outing, had to have basic knowledge of English, and had to make a formal request to be placed in an Outing. But Lily couldn't read, write, or speak English, and she never signed any kind of agreement. She was just sent out into the country to work, as she states in her Record Report of Carlisle Graduates and Return Students. It's interesting that Carlisle gave Lily this form to fill out, as she had never really been a student. Outing students also were required to attend school where they were placed for work. Lily never attended school during any of her outings.[18]

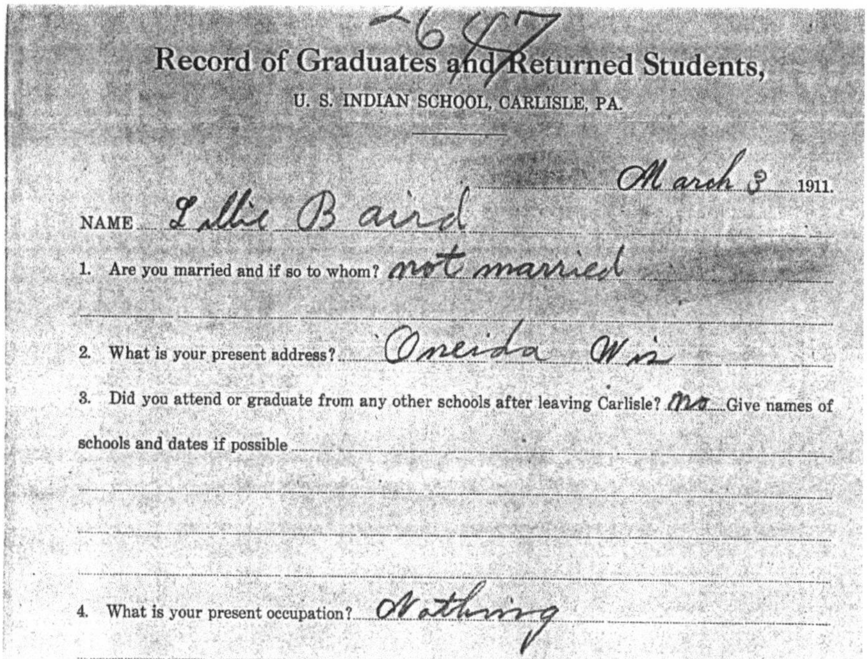

Record of Graduates and Returned Students,

U. S. INDIAN SCHOOL, CARLISLE, PA.

March 3 1911.

NAME *Lillie Baird*

1. Are you married and if so to whom? *not married*

2. What is your present address? *Oneida Wis*

3. Did you attend or graduate from any other schools after leaving Carlisle? *No* Give names of schools and dates if possible

4. What is your present occupation? *Nothing*

5. Tell something of your present home *I have no home*

6. What property in the way of land, stock, buildings, or money do you have? *I have no property no land I might as say I have nothing I have two cows*

7. Have you been in the Indian Service? In what positions? How long in each? *I never was in Indian Service I tell why it is I had no Schooling when I was to Carlisle I was send out in the country*

(Over)

Figure 4-Lily Huff-Baird filled out this report and sent it back to Carlisle Indian Industrial Boarding School in 1911, years after she had left the school. Charles A. Capasso photo.

The Outing Program at the Carlisle Indian Industrial Boarding School became very popular with white settlers, including Quakers, on the East Coast. There were more white people asking for students to work for them than there were students, always a surplus of white patrons wanting Indian students for employment. Based on their sex the girls would receive a wage of two to eight dollars a month and the boys five to fifteen dollars. I don't know if it was popular or posh or trendy for whites to employ Indian students as servants, but I do know that these Indian students provided cheap labor.[19]

Sophia spent about a year at the Carlisle Indian Industrial Boarding School, from July 8, 1891, to September 1892. Her NARA records state that she left July 6, 1897, for "time out," or having served five years at Carlisle; however, this record is incorrect.

In 2014 I found a photo of the Carlisle Indian Student Body posing on the school grounds. This photo was enlarged. Ironically, I had studied smaller images of this photo with a magnifying glass to try to find Sophia in this group. I was pleasantly surprised to actually find her in the enlarged photo at a Carlisle Symposium I attended in October. The photo fits the time period that Sophia was in attendance at Carlisle.

Figure 5-Sophia in School photo taken in March, 1892.
Focus on where Sophia is standing in group. Photo
courtesy of Cumberland County Historical Society.

Figure 6-Head shot of Sophia from this group picture, enhanced. Permission
to enhance photo from Cumberland County Historical Society.

After receiving her European-style clothing, hairdo, and shoes,
Sophia was surprised to see electric lights, indoor toilets, and water
running from indoor sinks and showers, all of which were progressive
technologies for that time[20] Sophia was hit many times for speaking
Oneida, which she had been speaking Oneida for fourteen and a half

years. Other children were punished for speaking their Indian languages too, the only languages they knew. English was literally beaten into the students. I found this horrific, outrageous, and discriminatory.

Because I had heard about Carlisle over the years and knew that Sophia had attended it, I had to go there to see this school for myself. My husband and I visited twice, first in June 2003. I was excited to see this place. The city of Carlisle itself is a quaint, old-fashioned town, and the school was a few miles away on the grounds of what is now the Army War College. When we arrived at the army base, we had to check in with guards before we were allowed onto the grounds. As we waited at the gates, I noticed a big blue sign with gold writing on it. Below it is shown in a black and white photo.

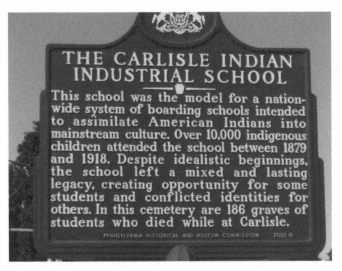

Figure 7-Carlisle Indian Industrial Boarding School
Cemetery sign. Photo courtesy of Charles A. Capasso

Figure 8-Cemetery. Photo courtesy of Charles A. Capasso

As we entered, I was shocked to see a small cemetery. All of the military-style marble or stone headstones looked new and had been engraved with children's names. The blue sign listed 186 graves in this tiny cemetery. I was sad and surprised to see that these were children. I wasn't sure why this cemetery was at the entrance or why it was on the grounds of the school that Sophia had attended. There had been no cemeteries on the grounds of schools I had attended. I wondered why students were buried here. What had caused their deaths here at Carlisle? This was all so strange to me. Later I learned that most Indian boarding schools in our country had cemeteries on them. The Indian children forced to attend them arrived with heavy hearts under much stress. Some of these kids died from homesickness. Others died from tuberculosis or smallpox. Many died from trying to run away from school, from the cold weather, starvation or being struck by a train. Some died eating foods they were not used to eating, malnourishment, and the results of abuse by the staff. Other kids most likely died from suicide. I read this during my research, and Grandma Millie also shared this with me. I was also shocked to learn that some of the children with TB and smallpox were sent home to die and to probably give their illnesses to their home tribe![21]

Before Sophia came to Carlisle in 1891 and after she left in 1892, children died at this school. Although the blue sign lists the 186 buried onsite, I have heard stories that hundreds more died at Carlisle than are buried in the tiny cemetery. No one really knows exactly how many children died at this school. No one! Records especially from Pratt's tenure, from 1879 to 1904, are often missing—perhaps because they were misplaced or just not kept—or inaccurate (i.e., falsified). How interesting that such a rigid military man as Pratt did not keep more accurate records on his students while he was in charge of Carlisle. Apparently he wanted to project to the US government and citizens that Carlisle was good and everything done there benefitted Native American children, even though most of them were forced to attend.

Very few records at NARA indicate the number of students who died at Carlisle, those that do show very few students (fewer than one hundred) as passing away there. Three lists record the deaths of Carlisle Indian students: the NARA record from the Carlisle Indian School, a list from Genevieve Bell and Barb Landis, and another list from another graduate student working on a thesis. A relative of mine learned that her aunt who attended Carlisle had died there, but there is no record of the aunt even attending Carlisle, much less dying at this school. However, the family was notified by Carlisle that the aunt had committed suicide at the school. That was all they were told. No explanation was given for why the aunt had killed herself. My relative told me that her aunt never would have killed herself.

When the US Army took over the Carlisle Indian School grounds, they moved the original cemetery to its present location and installed the military-type marble headstones on these graves. Rumor has it that not all of the children's bodies were actually moved to the new cemetery. I wondered about this. One story states that the remains of the children weren't relocated and that the original graveyard was just plowed over for a sports field and grandstand and then a building.[22] Another states that some of the buried bodies weren't moved and are now below an asphalt road. Another says that the original cemetery was much larger than the tiny one visitors see at the entrance gate today. No one has substantiated that bodies remained in their original locations, but a photo from the US Army Heritage and Education Center Digital Collections shows the brand-new cemetery, and a message written on the bottom of the photo reads, "New Cemetery ... The bodies of the Indians were removed to this site when the old cemetery-in rear of the grand stand had to be closed to make room for a new road." [23]

Out of respect for the dead, I would have kept the bodies where they were and put the new road somewhere else. There is plenty of other space on the Carlisle grounds where a new road could have been placed instead. I know this because I've walked those grounds twice now. I also found it interesting that there were some old headstones kept under lock and key in the basement of a building on the base. Why hide these? Apparently these headstones were found on the grounds of Carlisle by a landscaper, and the army collected them and locked them away from view.[24] I am sure those headstones are now long since destroyed or moved elsewhere. If I were the parent of one of these deceased children, I would have been devastated that my child had died at this school. I also would have wanted my child's body returned home so he or she could get a proper burial on the reservation. I am sure that some parents of children who died at Carlisle were never told why their children had died. Only God, our Creator, knows for sure how many children died at Carlisle and how many are actually entombed under the new asphalt road on the base.

Great-Grandma Sophie mentioned that some children died at Carlisle from abuse. I can't prove this, but I believe it's the truth. Sophia told Grandma Millie she was given lye soap to chew when she was caught speaking Oneida. She was also locked up, forced to scrub floors with a brush the size of a toothbrush on her hands and knees. She was also hit on her hands with a ruler for speaking Oneida. Is this not abuse? My Great-Grandma Sophia survived this abuse but never forgot it. I couldn't imagine Pratt or his staff sending a note to a parent telling that parent their child froze to death while trying to run away from Carlisle. No way were parents going to be informed that their children died from malnourishment, homesickness, or injuries from beatings, just as my relative never found out exactly how her aunt died at this school, just that she passed away from suicide. Native American Indians from across this country have come to pay their respects to these 186 children buried in this tiny cemetery. Since there are only three different lists of the number of children who died at Carlisle and since my relative's aunt's death was not recorded, I have no doubt that many other deaths were not reported.

As my husband and I continued walking around what used to be the Carlisle Indian School grounds, we learned that most of the buildings the school used are no longer standing. Carlisle is now home to the Army War College. I find it ironic that Carlisle was once used to train young army cavalry recruits to fight Native American Indians here in America and then, after being vacant for a while, reopened as the boarding school my ancestors attended.

Richard H. Pratt, an army captain, later named a General and veteran of the Indian Wars, became the first superintendent of the Carlisle Indian Industrial Boarding School in 1879. Prior to this position, he was the warden of Fort Marion Prison in St. Augustine, Florida, and in charge of seventy-two Indians incarcerated by the US government for killing white settlers, although it was never proven that these Indians killed white settlers.[25]

Thus, Pratt was not an educator. He was a military man. He ran Carlisle much like ran Fort Marion Prison—rigidly. Indian students were dealt harsh punishment for displaying any Indian tendencies. All the Indian children were to dress white, speak English, and become white, or else!

As we continued walking, we came upon an old building that I learned was once a guardhouse originally built during the Civil War as a prison. This building, called the Hessian Guardhouse, was also used by the Carlisle Indian School to jail students for misbehavior. Sophia may have been put here when she was locked up for speaking Oneida. This building contained four tiny cells, each with a very thick door that locked but no windows, so they were very dark. In one cell was a mannequin dressed in a Civil War uniform sitting on a thin bed. The upper lobby of the guardhouse displayed pictures of famous generals including Eisenhower, Bradley, and Westmoreland and a picture of the famous Jim Thorpe in his football uniform. There was also a huge black-and-white picture of the entire student body of Carlisle Indian School posing on the grounds in 1885. It was mentioned on a wall in the Hessian guardhouse that the Carlisle Indian School used the building from 1879 until 1918. The following was written on one of the walls in this building:

> Whether inhabitants were soldiers during the military operation of the post or Indian Students during the Indian School period, being confined here was not intended to be a pleasant experience. Today we can only wonder at the personalities who spent time here and the depth of emotion that was felt and expressed here. [26]

The Hessian Guardhouse as it looks today has few windows in it. The door to the building is very thick. Can you imagine being put into one of this building's dark cells just for being what you are, Oneida or Apache or Navajo or a member of any other Native American nation?

Figure 9-Hessian Guardhouse today. Photo courtesy of Charles A. Capasso

Since Pratt was the superintendent when Sophia attended Carlisle, she followed in other students' footsteps and had to march everywhere—to class, her dorm room, the dining hall, church services, her half-day domestic training session, and so on. Bells rang to signal that it was time to march to another class or part of the campus. Sophia was forbidden to leave the school grounds without chaperones. She could not visit her parents or Lily or any other Oneida Indians from Wisconsin, and her parents were discouraged from visiting Carlisle. Of course, most of these students' parents were too poor to afford the trip to Carlisle anyway. Carlisle staff read all the letters that children wrote home before sending them, so parents had no idea what was actually happening to their children. If a letter were written in the child's tribal language, it was not sent, and the child was punished for using his or her native tongue. No doubt these letters were destroyed immediately.

Sophia and the other students had no privacy. All were constantly monitored by staff, and some students were even asked to spy on the others. I compare this with a prison, where inmates are constantly watched by prison staff. When I attended school, I wasn't under constant watch, and I don't remember any of my schools being like a prison like Carlisle was. Children were released when they acted like white Americans and spoke only English. What kind of a school was that?

Sophia's dormitory was a three-story building that was situated right next to the school's bandstand. It has since been replaced by a tennis court, and a replica of the original bandstand sits near it. Supposedly, a man stood on this bandstand and watched everyone all the time. It was never revealed just who this man was, but the school newspaper, *The Indian Helper*, refers often to the "Man on the Bandstand," or MOTBS. A white matron at the school, Marianna Burgess, was in charge of the newspaper.[27]

According to *The Indian Helper*, the MOTBS could see the entire school grounds and into the buildings. He knew everything everyone was doing all the time. He had many powers. Why, he could even see all the Carlisle students on outings far away, even in other states! The newspaper wrote about this voyeur to intimidate and control the students; he was a tool for assimilation. His thoughts and views were printed weekly in the newspaper to tell the children that their Indian ways were savage and inferior. Reservation Indians were spoken of as dirty, lazy, stupid, and backward. I found these comments to be ignorant, vulgar, and discriminatory to the students and all Native American Indians.

The school published many different newspapers during its thirty-nine years of operation, including *The Red Man* (1888–1900), *The Redman and the Helper* (1880–1894), *The Indian Helper* (1885–1900), and *The Carlisle Arrow* (1904–1918). These newspapers reported on students' lives, their comings and goings at Carlisle, and their outings. Like *The Indian Helper*, some of these other newspapers were also used to control students with fear so that they could be assimilated into the white culture.

Reading these Carlisle newspapers, I couldn't help but think of Tokyo Rose, who broadcasted propaganda and lies to US troops during

World War II.[28] The MOTBS served the same purpose, shaming students for being Native American. How racist and repulsive! To degrade these Native American Indians their culture and heritage is outrageous.

Whoever MOTBS was, he had a very good view of everything, I noticed as I stood on the bandstand during our visit to the school grounds. I could envision Pratt standing on this bandstand. This reminded me of the watchtower of a prison, with Pratt the warden and the students the prisoners. As a student attending Carlisle I would've felt very uncomfortable and intimidated by this constant surveillance (or voyeurism). I would've wanted to crawl under a big rock and hide. Today there stands a replica of the original bandstand.

Figure 10-Replica of Bandstand today. Photo courtesy of Charles A. Capasso

The two-story white building with black shutters shown in the photo still stands. This was the teachers' residence and never housed students.

Since Sophia arrived at Carlisle only knowing how to speak Oneida, she was immediately put into a class to learn English. This class lasted half of her day, and in the other half of her day she learned sewing, laundry work, cooking, and cleaning, and she babysat the younger children on campus to prepare her for a servant's job when she left Carlisle permanently. She had many rules to follow and absolutely no choices. Her dorm room had to be kept clean and was inspected by Pratt and other staff weekly. She was organized into a military-type company and forced to drill on campus. She had to attend religious services weekly and pray every night.

All the students were viewed as inferior to the white people, incapable of becoming engineers, doctors, lawyers, or even Indian chiefs! So, they were taught only to be domestic servants and farm and factory hands. This labeling disgusted me immensely.

Even though Sophia had a beautiful singing voice, she never sang at Carlisle, neither receiving lessons nor singing in the choir. She was very frustrated and felt cheated because of this. She loved to sing! Yet Sophia was kept so busy that she had little time to think. Bells ran her life.

Sophia and the other students were given Carlisle's great order: "Do right." Sophia was taught that a "good Indian" followed the white man's ways. If Sophia kept her Indian ways, she was a "bad Indian." This makes me so angry I want to go back in time to tell off Pratt and his staff!

Sophia spent many lonely night missing her parents, Lily and her other siblings, and her Oneida home. She cried at night in her bed, as did many students. She had to cry very softly, she told Grandma Millie, so the matrons wouldn't hear her grieving, for she would be punished if they did. Carlisle students were never allowed to cry or show their true feelings when they missed their families. I find this terrible.

When Christmas came in 1891, neither Sophia nor Lily went home to Oneida as promised. Sophia spent Christmas at Carlisle along with many other students. She missed her family. She missed singing Oneida songs. She missed aroma, taste, and enjoyment of corn soup and fry bread. She missed talking in Oneida and the laughter and love she and her family shared at Christmas.

As far as academics were concerned, Carlisle apparently went up to eighth grade, although Sophia's academics never extended beyond learning English. The competency of the faculty was suspect. I cannot prove this. Some of the staff were hired because they knew Richard Pratt or had relatives or friends in charge of staffing Carlisle. Even Pratt wasn't an educator. Since Carlisle was really an experiment for Indian assimilation, education was not its focus.

Sophia, like all students, was assigned a number to identify her in Carlisle's records. Sophia's number was 2646. All of Carlisle's information about her outing, her tribe, her earnings from her outings, where she was from, her behavior, even comments on her physical stature, and records of her parents' names and her percentage of Indian blood was all recorded under number 2646, not her name. Sophia was just a number to Carlisle. When I learned about this, I couldn't help but think of prisoners in Nazi concentration camps, who had identifying numbers tattooed on their wrists.

Pratt occasionally gave students awards for going an extended time without speaking their native tongues. This left me nauseous. Sophia never received any of these awards. Instead, she was punished for getting caught speaking Oneida. Grandma Millie told me that Sophia's cageyness probably saved her from much more punishment.

When Sophia was at Carlisle, she and her fellow students celebrated the passage of the Dawes Act of 1887 as a holiday called Indian Citizenship Day. This law allotted Indian reservation lands to the Indians in hopes that they would learn to become farmers. It had absolutely nothing to do with Indians becoming American citizens. How ironic given that Indians were in this country long before the United States ever existed! This should have meant that we were already citizens and that those who served in the US government and other European settlers should have celebrated that they were the new citizens in this country.

Sophia also celebrated Thanksgiving at school as the "good" Indians who aided the brave Pilgrims. I have often thought about our Thanksgiving holiday over the years. Yes, Native American Indians did help the Pilgrims when they first arrived here in America. But history forgot to include that after the first Thanksgiving, Pilgrims and other non-Indian settlers moved Indians off their ancestral lands and onto lands reserved for them by the government so that their ancestral lands could be given to the settlers. I celebrate Thanksgiving to thank our Creator (God) that Native American Indians are still here and reviving their cultures and languages.

On New Year's Day, Sophia and her classmates celebrated the way white people kept track of time. On Washington's Birthday, they celebrated the "great white father's" birthday. On Memorial Day, they were made to decorate the graves of soldiers sent to kill their Indian fathers and mothers.

Below is Sophia's schedule at Carlisle.

Morning:
6:00 a.m.: Rising Bell and Reveille
6:15 a.m.: Assembly Call
6:35 a.m.: Mess Call and Breakfast Bell
7:25 a.m.: Work Whistle
8:35 a.m.: School Bell
11:30 a.m.: Recall Bell from School
11:30 a.m.: Recall Whistle from Work
11:45 a.m.: Assembly Call
11:55 a.m.: Mess Call and Dinner Bell

Afternoon:
12:55 p.m.: Work Whistle
1:10 p.m.: School Bell

4:00 p.m.: Recall Bell from School

4:00 p.m.: Recall Whistle from Work

5:45 p.m.: Flag Salute

6:00 p.m.: Supper Bell

7:30 p.m.: Evening Hour

8:45 p.m.: Bell for Roll Call and Prayer

9:00 p.m.: Bell for Assembly

9:30 p.m.: Taps and Inspection of Rooms

"Wow, Sophia was very much regimented at Carlisle and had little time to think!"

Quakers and abolitionists were benefactors of the school. Members of these groups would visit Carlisle often to see how the students' assimilation, particularly their conversion to Christianity, was coming along. I was appalled that Sophia was at this school to become white and have her soul saved because she was considered a savage.

I am somewhat relieved that Sophia did not speak nor understand English when she first arrived at Carlisle because it meant that she couldn't read the school newspapers printed there. For example, *The Indian Helper* ran an article on Friday, April 8, 1892, titled "Killing the Indian and How We Must Kill Him." The headline alone makes me queasy. This article is about making Indians forget their own languages and cultures. I know Sophia would've been heartsick if she had been able to read it. We Indians were considered savages and therefore had to be killed. We were considered inhuman. No wonder I grew up rooting for the white cowboys to kill the Indians. I wasn't some wild, inhuman beast!

I'm sure the US government saw Elizabeth as a threat because she refused to assimilate into white culture, and Indians who were considered threats like her often had their children, in this case Sophia and Lily, removed from their homes. I felt very sad that Sophia and

Lily were taken from their parents and sent to Carlisle. This was not right. Other children related to their tribal leaders or chiefs were also removed from their homes. This makes me want to cry. The government did all this to control Elizabeth and tribal heads and chiefs, part of the assimilation process. Some Indian children removed from their homes were assimilated to the point that they could not speak their native tongues with their parents, relatives, and friends when they did return to their reservations, which is very sad.

As mentioned, Sophia's dormitory has been replaced by a tennis court, but the two-story teachers' residence still stands. A plaque on the wall currently says it was the girls' dormitory, but no girls ever resided there.

I sincerely thank my Grandma Millie and other relatives for sharing with me what Sophia's experience at Carlisle was really like. Grandma Millie said that the US government no doubt thought that assimilating the feisty Sophia Huff was akin to breaking a wild horse.

In September of 1892, Sophia and a group of other Indian girls were summoned into a large room and told to stand in a straight line. A group of white ladies then entered the room. Just as Lily had the year before, Sophia stood still as these white ladies walked up and down the line, looking over each girl carefully. Most of these women were Quakers, and all of them were from the East Coast. As Grandma Millie told me this story, I couldn't help but think of the white plantation owners looking over African Americans standing on stage for sale at slave auctions in the South.

One Quaker lady pointed to Sophia and said in English, "I will take her as my servant." Sophia knew very little English, so she didn't understand the lady, but Carlisle's matrons did. Sophia had been chosen to live in this lady's home in New Jersey and work as a servant. Sophia had been at Carlisle only one year. Her choosing, like Lily's, ran contrary to Carlisle's rule that "outings were only for students who had a basic understanding of English. Also, students supposedly were not forced into an outing experience and were instead to make a formal request for placement. Lily couldn't speak a word of English prior to her outing, Sophia could barely speak English, and neither of them had made formal requests to be placed in an outing and thus were forced into their placements. Many other students had this same experience. Despite that they had been placed in menial jobs outside of Carlisle; they were still listed as students at Carlisle.

The Outing Program was very desirable to non-Indian settlers, including the Quakers, and Pratt loved it. His students' placements with white families was the ultimate way to assimilate them into white culture, and the students were required to send half to two-thirds of their earnings back to the school for safe keeping.[29] Thus Pratt was making money not only from the government, which paid per student attending the school, but also from the students themselves. With the popularity of having Indian students as workers among white European settlers and the cheap cost for their labor, you can see why Lily was sent right out to work without ever attending school.

Sophia was told she would be with this Quaker family for a year or two. Another of Carlisle's rule was that students would spend only a summer, one year, or two years on an outing. Again this was not the case for Sophia, Lily, or many other students. Below are copies of two records of Sophia's outings. The first is dated July 8, 1891, when Sophia first arrived at Carlisle. This record has been falsified. Sophia wasn't released from Carlisle due to time out. Instead, she was working in outing as a servant to Mary and Abel Tomlinson in New Jersey. The second record has also been falsified. Sophia didn't return to Carlisle in August 1897. She continued working as a servant for the Tomlinson's. She also didn't work for the Haines family in Moorestown, New Jersey. Last, she was never legally adopted by the Tomlinson's.

CARLISLE INDIAN INDUSTRIAL SCHOOL.
DESCRIPTIVE AND HISTORICAL RECORD OF STUDENT.   *over*

ENGLISH NAME	AGENCY	NATION
763 Sophia Huff	Green Bay, Wis	Oneida

BAND	INDIAN NAME	HOME ADDRESS
		Nicholas Huff.

PARENTS LIVING OR DEAD	BLOOD	AGE	HEIGHTH	WEIGHT	FORCED INSP.	FORCED EXPR.	SEX.
FATHER: Living MOTHER: Living	Full	14	4 10½		30	27½	F.

ARRIVED AT SCHOOL	FOR WHAT PERIOD	DATE DISCHARGED	CAUSE OF DISCHARGE
July 8, 1891	5 years.	July 6, 1897	Time out.

TO COUNTRY	PATRONS NAME AND ADDRESS		FROM COUNTRY
Sep. 8, 92	M. Tomlinson	Rancocas N.J.	Sep. 13, 93
Oct. 12, 93	Mrs. F. Haines	Moorestown "	Transf,

SHAW-WALKER MUSKEGON 6478

Admitted 2646

CARLISLE INDIAN INDUSTRIAL SCHOOL.
DESCRIPTIVE AND HISTORICAL RECORD OF STUDENT.

NUMBER	ENGLISH NAME	AGENCY	NATION
1281	Sophia Huff	Oneida, Wis.	Oneida

BAND	INDIAN NAME	HOME ADDRESS
		Nicholas Huff

PARENTS LIVING OR DEAD	BLOOD	AGE	HEIGHTH	WEIGHT	FORCED INSP.	FORCED EXPR.	SEX.
FATHER: Living MOTHER: Living	Full	21	5-1	135	33½	31	F.

ARRIVED AT SCHOOL	FOR WHAT PERIOD	DATE DISCHARGED	CAUSE OF DISCHARGE
Aug. 28, 1897	5 years.	Sept. 15, 1898	Adopted in family

TO COUNTRY	PATRONS NAME AND ADDRESS		FROM COUNTRY
Aug 30, 97	M. Tomlinson	Rancocas N.J.	Sep. 16, 98

SHAW-WALKER MUSKEGON 6478

Figure 11-Two Carlisle Indian School Records
of Sophia J. Huff. NARA Records

After Sophia was told she was leaving Carlisle to be a servant in New Jersey, she was excused to go to her dorm room to pack her things. She packed whatever clothes and undergarments Carlisle had given her into a trunk and headed back to the room full of Quaker ladies and Carlisle staff. Mary Tomlinson, a Quaker lady from Rancocas/Laurel Springs, New Jersey, motioned to Sophia to follow her to the Carlisle School Train Depot. Sophia obeyed but was very scared. She couldn't communicate very well with Mary Tomlinson and didn't know her from Adam, yet she was now headed to work for the Tomlinson family. Mary seemed kind enough, but Sophia remained cautious and reserved on the train. She heard the whistle blow as the train chugged out of the station. Sophia never returned to the Carlisle Indian Industrial Boarding School, not even to visit, according to the school's visitors' book.

Of the 10,000 to 12,000 students who attended Carlisle from 1879 to 1918, only 761 approximately graduated. I say approximately because various other references list varying numbers for total students graduating from Carlisle. There really isn't any actual, accurate number of graduates from Carlisle., I wondered what the criteria for graduation was and found some insight in a speech Rev. A. J. Lippincott gave to Carlisle students at the "1898 graduation ceremony".: "The Indian is DEAD in you. Let all that is Indian within you DIE! You cannot truly become American citizens, industrious, intelligent, cultured and civilized until the INDIAN WITHIN YOU IS DEAD!" After the reverend's speech, Pratt jumped to his feet and said loudly, "I have never fired a bigger shot and never hit the bull's eye more center!" After I read this, I realized that the only criterion was assimilation.

When graduates left Carlisle, they received a book called *Stiya, pseudonym Embe,* by Marion Burgess, a white matron at Carlisle for many years and head of the school newspapers. This book is about a young Pueblo girl, Stiya, who returns to the Pueblo reservation after attending Carlisle. She is shocked by what she sees on the reservation.

She finds the tribe wild, dirty, and unkempt and their environment unsanitary: she is repulsed by the sight of raw meat hanging out in the open to dry with flies all over it. This propaganda book published by the US Army in 1891 was an attempt to keep Carlisle students from returning to their Indian ways after graduation. I was repulsed by the racism and lies Burgess wrote about Stiya and her tribe. I was shocked that the US Army published this book and that the US government paid to have these books mailed to Carlisle graduates. Sophia, having never graduated, did not receive a copy of *Stiya*, thank God!

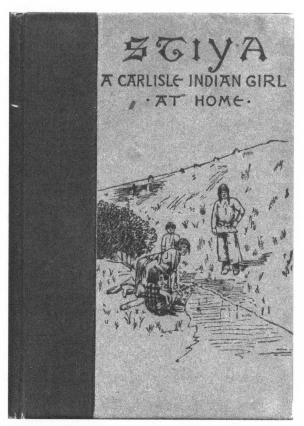

Figure 12-Picture of original book, STIYA, which was mailed to Carlisle Indian School Graduates to further the assimilation process. Photo courtesy of Charles A. Capasso

Sophia's Outing: September 1892 to June 1902

T he train ride from Carlisle to New Jersey was not very long, unlike the trip from Oneida, Wisconsin, to Carlisle, Pennsylvania. The train soon slowed, a whistle blew, and the train stopped completely. Sophia was very uncomfortable not knowing where she now was. Mary motioned for Sophia to follow her out the train door. Sophia stepped onto the platform and noticed the beautiful countryside and the changing colors of the leaves on this September day in 1892. Mary waved at a white gentleman sitting in a horse-drawn buggy. This was Abel Tomlinson, Mary's husband. He had come to the train depot in Rancocas/Laurel Springs to pick up his wife and new servant, Sophia.

Sophia smiled cautiously next to Mary in the buggy as Abel drove. She was now far removed from the militaristic rigidity of the Carlisle Indian Industrial Boarding School. She was no longer surrounded by a high fence or under constant surveillance. She now was with a white Quaker family in a different state. All of this was foreign to her, but she and the Tomlinson's managed to live together for the next ten years, until June 1902. As noted in the last chapter, although NARA records state that Sophia attended other outings, she was discharged from Carlisle after five years on July 6, 1897, for time out, returned to Carlisle on August 28, 1897, and then went on another outing on August 30, 1897. This information is false, having been made up by the Carlisle staff. Sophia's only outing was her ten years spent serving Mary and Abel Tomlinson in New Jersey, according to Grandma Millie and the Carlisle school newspaper *The Red Man and the Helper*, which printed an article in June 1902 about Sophia being a servant of good standing to the Tomlinson's for the previous ten years.

Grandma Millie told me the Tomlinson's treated Sophia kindly, saying, "Well, these Quakers were Sophia's family now. They taught Sophia English and the Quaker ways of life."

When I was a child, Grandma Millie mentioned that her mother had lived with a Quaker family in Pennsylvania, and I often wondered why Sophia lived with this family so far away from Oneida, Wisconsin, but no one ever explained her situation. After visiting Carlisle and talking to Grandma Millie, I wanted to learn more about Sophia's life with the Tomlinson's and why she had left Carlisle after only one year in school and lived with the Tomlinson's for ten years. I also wanted to see the house Sophia lived in with Mary and Abel all those years.

Records from NARA didn't give the exact address but did note that it was in Laurel Springs and Rancocas, New Jersey, and not Pennsylvania, as Grandma Millie and the rest of my family thought. I went through outing records of various other students and saw that they all listed only the cities and states where students worked and not their exact addresses, thus making it was extremely difficult to find the Tomlinson's' home, but I was on a mission to find it.

In 2007 my husband, Chick, and I traveled to Laurel Springs, New Jersey, in hopes of finding the Tomlinson's' house. We drove around the town for a while and stopped at a home that had a sign in front that said "Tomlinson Home." It was closed for renovations into a museum. We then stopped at a YMCA building that had once been another Tomlinson home. Neither of these were the home Sophia lived in. We talked to a YMCA employee who told us of another Tomlinson home just down the road, and he gave us the address. Sure enough, this huge

Victorian house had once been occupied by a Tomlinson family. As Chick and I parked our car, I thought that descendants of the Abel and Mary Tomlinson may still be living there.

As we exited the car, I spotted a middle-aged man watering plants in the backyard. I was a bit apprehensive to bother him, but Chick and I did approach him and ask him if he knew whether the Tomlinson family lived there. We were pleasantly surprised that this man, who introduced himself as Geoff Smith, was actually a descendant of the Tomlinson family. His mother, Cora Barbara (Walker) Smith, was in her late eighties and still resided in this house, and her aunt and uncle were Mary and Abel Tomlinson. Geoff kindly invited us inside the house to meet his mother, who wanted us to call her Barbara. They talked to us for a while about the Indian girl from Carlisle that once lived in this home with Barbara's mother (Cora Tomlinson Walker) and grandparents (Ephraim and Sara Tomlinson). Cora befriended this Indian girl who, surprisingly, was not Sophia Huff but another girl named Grace Thumbo, an Apache-Mohave Indian sent from Carlisle. Geoff and Barbara said that Grace spent several years as the family's servant. NARA records indicated that she lived with the Tomlinson's only one year, but this is not true. Below is a photo of Grace given to me by Barbara Tomlinson. On the back of this photo was inscribed: Grace Thumbo, Mohave Tribe, A sweet girl who lived with us for several years. It is signed by Cora T. Walker, Barbara's mother. Since Carlisle's records on my great grandmother Sophie were falsified, there is no doubt in my mind that Grace's records were also falsified. I am 100% sure Barbara and Geoff Smith told me the truth about Grace. They even showed me an Indian doll Grace made and sent to Cora as a gift. Barbara cherishes this doll even today at the age of 97!

Figure 13-Photo of Grace Thumbo. Photo courtesy of Barbara and Geoff Smith, relatives of Tomlinson Family.

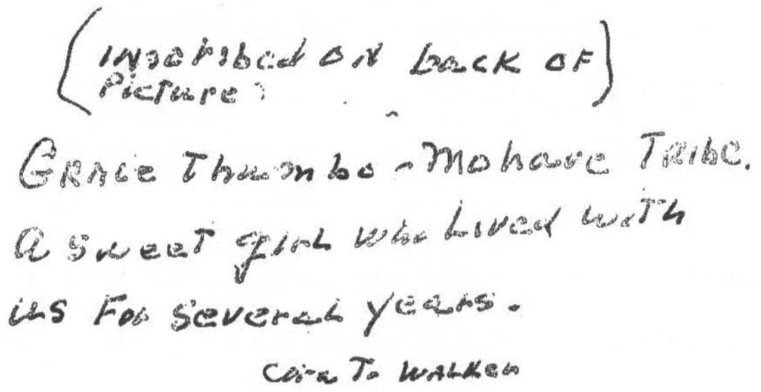

(Inscribed on back of)
Picture)

Grace Thumbo - Mohave Tribe.
A sweet girl who lived with
us for several years.

Cora T. Walker

Figure 14-Photo of inscription on back picture of Grace, written by the Tomlinson Family at the turn of the century. Scanned by Charles A. Capasso

Barbara asked me if I knew anything of what became of Grace after she left her outing with Ephraim and Sara Tomlinson in the early 1900s. I told Barbara that I really didn't know anything about Grace, but that I was shocked to find out about another Indian student from Carlisle working as a servant away from the boarding school. Geoff and Barbara told us that Grace was listed on the 1900 census of New Jersey as being a servant for the family, which meant that she had been adopted into the family. Apparently many white families in Laurel Springs and

Rancocas and the surrounding towns employed Carlisle students as servants during this time, and Grace knew other Indian girls from Carlisle working in the area.

Barbara told us that her uncle Abel and Aunt Mary lived in the area when they were alive, but she did not have their exact address during our visit. I thought about Sophia living with Abel and Mary from 1892 until 1902, and although we couldn't confirm this, I was sure that Grace and Sophia would have crossed paths because their employers were relatives. Little did I know at that time that Grace and Sophia lived only about a mile from each other!

Chick and I learned a lot from our visit with Barbara and Geoff, and we thanked them for sharing their precious family history. I promised them I would try to find out more about Grace Thumbo, and Barbara said she planned to find exactly where Abel, Mary, and Sophia lived. She and Geoff also suggested that we talk to Bob and Mary Tomlinson, other relatives of theirs, so Chick and I headed to Bob and Mary's. They graciously shared information about the Tomlinson family genealogy with us.

Grandma Millie told me that Sophia had lived with Abel and Mary in a redbrick two-story house. Sophia had her own bedroom above a screened back porch.

After seeing Carlisle twice, seeing the towns of Laurel Springs and Rancocas, and meeting the Barbara and Geoff and Mary and Bob, by August of 2007 Barbara Smith sent me a letter and two pictures. In her letter she gave the address of the house where Abel and Mary lived with Sophia and explained that she and Geoff had walked the mile from their home to the other Tomlinson house, whose present owners, Sandy and Ken Johnson, allowed her to take some pictures and chatted. Wow! I had finally found the house where Sophia had actually lived for ten years, and it was still standing and had people living in it! As I looked at the two picture of this home, I realized how sharp minded my now

101-year-old grandma Millie was, although she had been wrong about Sophia's living in Pennsylvania. We all were wrong about that in my family. Her description of the house was 100 percent right! I was thrilled to finally know where Sophia had spent her ten-year outing.

After further research, I also learned more about what had happened to Grace Thumbo. NARA records mentioned that she had gone to other outings after having served the Tomlinson's for a year and that she was released from Carlisle because of time served as a student. These records were falsified by Carlisle staff like records about other students. Grace did go home to California in September 1904. However, she never attended any other outings besides that with the Tomlinson's, and she wasn't released from Carlisle for time served. Instead, her brother traveled from California to Laurel Springs, New Jersey, to bring his sister back from Ephraim, Sara, and Cora Tomlinson's home. He did this because he did not want Grace to be assimilated into white culture.

In 1905 Grace had a son named William while living at Camp McDowell, Arizona, a reservation for the Mohave-Apache, Yuma-Apache, and Tonto-Apache Indian tribes. Camp McDowell is now known as Fort McDowell. Grace later moved to Phoenix, Arizona, and had two more children. I tried to find her relatives and descendants to learn more, but unfortunately, I was not able to. I shared what information I had with Barbara and Geoff, who were happy to learn about what had become of Grace Thumbo after she had left the Tomlinson's in 1904.[30]

Now that I had learned about the redbrick house where Sophia lived for ten years with the Tomlinson's, I yearned to see it. I researched it on the Internet and found information about it from the Camden County, New Jersey, Historical Society in New Jersey indicating that it had been built in 1742 and that an addition had been built in 1798. The two-story house, called "The Brick House Farm" or "The Old Place," originally sat on 619 acres of land. This land included a grist mill and a farm owned by the Tomlinson family, who also owned other grist mills in the area.

Benjamin Tomlinson, Abel's grandfather, had built the house, and his son, James, and James's children, Abel and Hannah, had been born there. Abel and Hannah grew up there. When James Tomlinson died in 1871, this house and all the land were deeded to Abel and Hannah, who divided the property. Abel took the eastern end, which consisted of about 337 acres on which sat the house, farm, and grist mill, and Hannah, who was now married, took the remaining acreage. Abel and his wife, Mary, lived in this house with Sophia from 1892 until 1902. Sophia had gone from a very poor home on a poor Native American Indian reservation in Oneida, Wisconsin, to an Indian boarding school in Carlisle, Pennsylvania, to the home of a white Quaker English-speaking family in the countryside of New Jersey to live as a servant, all in one year. What a contrast!

In the summer of 2012, Chick and I toured this house. I thank the current residents—Ken and Sandy Johnson; their three sons, Chris, Nick, and Kevin; and their dog, Junior; and bird, a Sparrow named Ernesto, for allowing us to see inside this home where my great-grandma Sophia worked as a servant for ten years. Many emotions ran through me as I saw it. It was overwhelming, and I had to bite my lip to keep from crying. I truly could feel Sophia's presence.

The first photo of the house is from the turn of the century and shows, on the right, a stable that was once attached to home. According to the present residents, this view is actually the back of the house. The back door leads to the kitchen, where Sophia did a lot of cooking and cleaning.

Figure 15-Tomlinson Home at turn of the 20th century. Photo by Charles A. Capasso

Figure 16-Tomlinson House as it looks today. Photo by Charles A. Capasso

The stable is now long gone. Just as Grandma Millie had mentioned, it did have a back porch with a room above it. Today, 90 percent of the house has been restored to its original late-1740s state. The only differences now are indoor bathrooms and updated appliances in the kitchen.

Walking into this house was like going back in time. Inside the house there were two sets of stairs: one for the owners and the other for the servants. The Johnsons told us that Sophia and other servants slept in the tiny rooms that were located on the second floor, in the middle of the house. Abel and Mary had separate quarters that servants were not allowed into unless they were cleaning them or serving food to the owners and guests. Sophia cooked, cleaned the house, and sewed all the clothes for the Tomlinson's, and in her later years, she spent a lot of time supervising newer servants. As I climbed the steep, narrow servants' stairway, I imagined Sophia and the other servants climbing them too and was glad Sophia was so tiny. I am much bigger than she was. I found the stairs difficult to navigate. Those stairs went from the kitchen on the first floor to the servants' quarters on the second floor, with access to the owners' bedrooms too.

Figures 17-Photo of the Servants' narrow, steep stairs located in the middle of the house. Photo courtesy of Charles A. Capasso
Figure 18-Photo of stairs. Photo by Charles A. Capasso

What is now a small bedroom on the first floor was the summer kitchen when Sophia lived there. Because the main kitchen had no air conditioning, it would get too hot in the summer, so servants used the summer kitchen because it had windows and a back door to let in cool air. The yard also featured a number of outhouses over the years.

I sat in a chair in one of the tiny bedrooms where Sophia would have slept and was overwhelmed with emotion. This small bedroom had an original old wall lamp in one corner and a small window overlooking the yard and creek outside. The Johnsons told me that the servants slept in small beds, and the room was so tiny that only a small bed would fit in it. Because Sophia was so small herself, the tiny bedroom fit her. Here am I, in a chair, peering out the window of one of bedrooms Sophia would have slept in. I could feel her presence as I sat in the little room.

Figure 19-Me sitting in one of Sophia's tiny bedrooms.
Photo courtesy Charles A. Capasso

As Ken and Sandy Johnson continued the tour, they pointed out that all the floors were the original floors from the 1740s and that the furniture in the owners' quarters was all from that period too. Even the walls had been painted in colors popular at that time. Though the kitchen had had some updating with modern appliances and indoor plumbing, it still featured a huge hearth and fireplace that had been used for all the cooking. The summer kitchen had a similar but smaller fireplace that had also been used for cooking.

Abel Tomlinson had lived in this house most of his life, and he even passed away there, in the dining room, the Johnsons had said. He was born in this house to James and Rachel Haines Tomlinson in 1840, and he went on to serve in the Civil War from 1863 until 1865. After leaving military service, he met and married Mary B. Allen from Solesbury, Pennsylvania. He and Mary had a daughter named Anna Carrie Tomlinson. Sadly, Anna died in infancy in the late 1860s. Having inherited the grist mill, farm, and house from his father in 1871, Abel was a miller and farmer and was very wealthy because he owned 337 acres of land.

The Tomlinson's were good to Sophia, Grandma Millie told me. According to the 1900 US Census, Sophia was a servant living with Abel and Mary Tomlinson, and her race is listed as Indian [White]. Like Grace Thumbo's, Sophia's listing as a servant on this census meant that she had been adopted by Abel and Mary, although this adoption was never made legal. Carlisle even went so far as to put "adopted out" on Sophia's school records. It really bothered me that Sophia's status as servant was considered equivalent to adoption. Let's face it: Sophia was not adopted; she was a *servant*, and although she also was listed as white on the census, she was 100 percent Oneida Indian.

Two records have been reproduced. The first is of Sophia's second record card from Carlisle, which shows "Adopted in family," and the bottom is the 1900 Census record that lists Sophia is listed as a servant and as white.

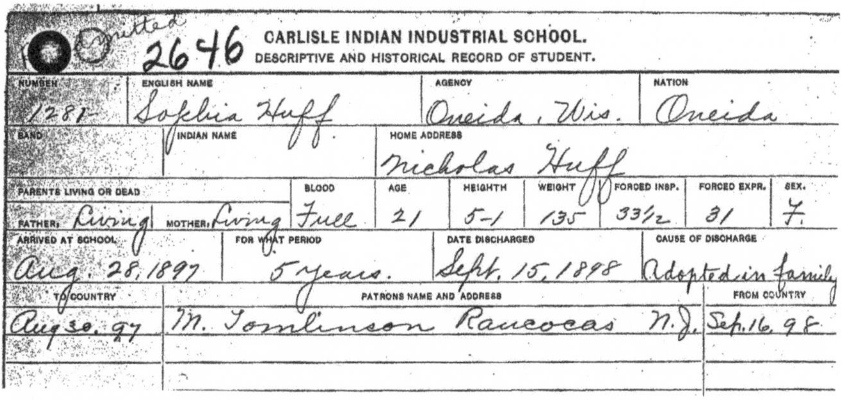
2646

CARLISLE INDIAN INDUSTRIAL SCHOOL.
DESCRIPTIVE AND HISTORICAL RECORD OF STUDENT.

NUMBER	ENGLISH NAME	AGENCY	NATION
1281	Sophia Huff	Oneida, Wis.	Oneida

BAND	INDIAN NAME	HOME ADDRESS
		Nicholas Huff

PARENTS LIVING OR DEAD	BLOOD	AGE	HEIGHTH	WEIGHT	FORCED INSP.	FORCED EXPR.	SEX.
FATHER, Living MOTHER, Living	Full	21	5-1	135	33½	31	F.

ARRIVED AT SCHOOL	FOR WHAT PERIOD	DATE DISCHARGED	CAUSE OF DISCHARGE
Aug. 28, 1897	5 years.	Sept. 15, 1898	Adopted in family

TO COUNTRY	PATRONS NAME AND ADDRESS	FROM COUNTRY
Aug 30. 97	M. Tomlinson Rancocas N.J.	Sep. 16. 98

Figure 20-photo of Sophia's second Carlisle Outing Record Card, which shows written: "Adopted in family." Courtesy NARA

1900 United States Federal Census

Name:	**Sophia J Huff**
Home in 1900:	**Willingborough, Burlington, New Jersey**
Age:	**23**
Birth Date:	**Nov 1876**
Birthplace:	**Wisconsin**
Race:	**Indian** *(Native American)* **[White]**
Ethnicity:	**American**
Relationship to head-of-house:	**Servant**
Father's Birthplace:	**Wisconsin**
Mother's Birthplace:	**Wisconsin**
Marital Status:	**Single**
Residence :	**Willingborough Township, Burlington, New Jersey**
Occupation:	View Image
Neighbors:	View others on page

Household Members:

Name	Age
Atal H Tomlinson	59
Mary A Tomlinson	57
Sophia J Huff	23

Figure 21-photo of New Jersey 1900 Census Record that lists Sophia as a servant and as white.

Mary taught Sophia how to cook Quaker and other European-derived foods, how to speak and write English, and how to sew, crochet, and knit. Grandma Millie said that Sophia was also sent to a sewing school nearby so she could learn to make and mend clothes for the Tomlinson's. Sophia attended Methodist Sunday school, although she had been baptized Episcopal as an infant in Oneida in 1877. Sophia did not attend regular school during her time with the Tomlinson's. She did only what Carlisle had taught her to do: be a servant. She cleaned, cooked, sewed, prayed daily, and followed other Quaker practices. She waited on Mary and Abel at mealtimes. Sophia wore Victorian-style dresses, was not allowed to swear or drink alcohol, and she had to attend church services every Sunday. I learned that Sophia was a leader in a group called the White Ribbon Band. I know that she could not play any musical instruments, but she had a beautiful sing voice and loved to sing, so she most likely sang in the group upon learning to speak English. I am sure she enjoyed being in this group. She was called a "leader" of the Sabbath school, which meant that she babysat the Quakers' children while their parents were in church.

When Sophia came to live with the Tomlinson's, she came to a home with no electricity or indoor plumbing, which she felt somewhat comfortable with because her log home in Oneida had had similar amenities. Privies (outhouses) were the norm, as was collecting rainwater in barrels for washing clothes and bathing. Water for drinking and cooking came from a hand pump outside, which Sophia had never seen before. There was a window box protruding from a kitchen window for storing a block of ice, delivered weekly by the iceman. This box of ice was used to keep foods that needed to be cool, preserved.

Continuing the tour, Chick and I noticed that the house was located near Laurel Lake and Timber Creek in a beautiful area. Near the creek, now overgrown, was a path to the grist mill, which no longer stands. An earlier relative of Abel's, Ephraim Tomlinson, built homes for the mill's workers and a school for the workers' children to attend. I thought that was thoughtful of him, and this showed that The Tomlinson's cared about their employees and treated all of them, including Sophia, well.

Carlisle staff periodically checked on students working at outings to make sure they were doing good work. Pratt himself liked to keep tabs on how his students were fairing with the white families they were placed with.

I have wondered why Sophia stayed with Abel and Mary for so long. Yes, the Tomlinson's were good to her, and Sophia was a hardworking servant. She respected the Tomlinson's and they respected her. They even claimed that they had adopted her by listing her as a servant on the 1900 Federal Census and as "adopted in family" on September 15, 1897, on her Carlisle record. But Sophia wasn't legally adopted. Instead, she was more like an indentured servant, expected to permanently stay with Abel and Mary as their servant. There is no doubt in my mind that Sophia stayed with Abel and Mary for ten years to avoid any repercussions from the Carlisle Indian Industrial School, to avoid causing any trouble for her parents from the US government. She was afraid of the consequences for going home to Oneida without permission from the Tomlinson's or Carlisle to do so. That Sophia would even need permission to visit her parents in Oneida bothers me in itself.

Sophia missed her family, home, and friends in Wisconsin. She wasn't allowed to speak her native language, and she wasn't allowed to go to her real home in Oneida.

Over the ten years she spent in New Jersey, Sophia became fluent in English, even learning to write in English very well. The Tomlinson's taught Sophia a lot and were very fond of her, and she was very grateful to them. She eventually became the Tomlinson's' head servant, supervising the many new servants who came to work for the Tomlinson's during her tenure.

In late June of 1902, Abel and Mary Tomlinson allowed Sophia to travel back to Oneida, Wisconsin, to visit for a few months. After the summer was over, Sophia was to return to New Jersey and serve Abel and Mary permanently. Sophia was happy to know she was going to go back and visit family on the Oneida Reservation. Grandma Millie says Sophia sang to herself around the Tomlinson's home as she was working. She was so thrilled! With eleven years gone by, Sophia was no longer the fourteen year old teenager her parents saw being forcefully taken away from them in July, 1891. She was now a grown woman!

Carlisle Indian Industrial Boarding School's *The Red Man and the Helper* explains in its July 4, 1902, issue:

> Sophia Hoff [*sic*] and Jemima Schanandore [Skenandore] have gone home to Oneida, Wisconsin for the summer. They both have good homes in New Jersey and have proved so efficient they will remain indefinitely. Sophia has lived ten years with Mary and Abel Tomlinson at Rancocas, New Jersey, where she is a member of the Methodist Church, a leader in the White Ribbon Band and a leader of the Sabbath School.

I do not know whether Abel and Mary or Sophia herself paid the train fare. In any event, on June 27, 1902, Sophia Huff and Jemima Skenandore boarded a train headed west to Oneida, Wisconsin.

Sophia Returns to Oneida, Wisconsin

Sophia and Jemima were so excited to get on the train to Oneida that late June day in 1902, and their hearts raced as the train slowly moved out of the depot. The trip would take at least three days, but the girls didn't care, as they were so happy they were going to finally see their families again. Jemima grinned at Sophia and whispered something in Oneida to her schoolmate. Soon both girls were whispering in Oneida, careful not to draw the conductor's or other passengers' attention.

Sophia and Jemima were full of emotions. Sophia, after being away eleven years, was now older and dressed in Victorian attire, and Jemima, too, was totally different in dress and appearance.

Sophia looked down at her hard-toed government-issued shoes. *Boy, it sure would be comfortable to have a pair of moccasins on right now,* she thought. She looked forward to seeing Elizabeth, Nicholas, and her siblings. She and Jemima talked incessantly in Oneida to make the train ride seem shorter. After a few days, the girls heard the train slowing down. The trip, which included a stop to switch trains in Chicago, to catch the Green Bay and Western train, had tired them.

Figure 22-Oneida Train Depot as it looked in 1902 when Sophia and Jemima returned to Wisconsin. Photo courtesy of the Oneida Museum.

The big locomotive barely chugged, and finally, it came to a complete stop. Sophia wondered whether she would even recognize her parents or siblings or whether they might not recognize her. She also wondered if she would finally see her sister Lily. She was unaware she would meet a new sister, Mary, who had been born after Sophia was sent away to Carlisle. Many questions and feelings flooded Sophia's mind as the train stopped at the Oneida Depot.

Sophia hugged Jemima, and then both ladies reached for their suitcases. Sophia's heart beat a mile a minute as she started walking toward the train door. She nervously stepped onto the station platform and looked around for her family. She soon spotted her mother, Elizabeth, and her father, Nicholas, standing together.

Elizabeth looked up at Sophia, dressed in Victorian clothes and wearing her hair up in a bun. She had never seen Sophia dressed like this or with her hair like this before. She was no longer the teenager who had been taken away in 1891. Elizabeth studied Sophia as she approached, clutching her suitcase. Sophia saw clearly that her parents had aged. Nicholas now wore overalls over a shirt, and Elizabeth wore a printed cotton dress, which she had most likely sewn herself, and moccasins.

Sophia suddenly held out her arms and greeted her parents in Oneida, and everyone broke down in tears, sobbing as they hugged each other tightly. Elizabeth no longer cared how her daughter wore her hair or which clothes her daughter wore, for Sophia's use of Oneida told her and Nicholas that Sophia had not lost her Oneida heritage despite being kept away for eleven long years. Their daughter was home!

Sophia and her parents then slowly made their way to a horse-drawn wagon that was most likely borrowed from a neighbor, and then Nicholas drove them to Elizabeth's log home on Salt Pork Avenue in Oneida. Grandma Millie told me the street had gotten its name from the smell of salt pork, then a staple for the Oneidas, cooking in the homes along it. Ironically, Elizabeth rented the log home from a white settler named E. P. Boland, who had built a block of small homes on land he had purchased from an Oneida and now rented out to Oneidas.[31]

Sophia surveyed her surroundings. A multitude of poor, dilapidated houses, small log cabins, and wooden shacks now occupied the Oneida Reservation, and the reservation was smaller than it had been when she left. Many white settlers now owned much of the land since the passage of the Dawes Act of 1887. By 1906, this law had divided reservations in the United States into separately owned properties. The goal of this allotment had been to turn reservation trust land into private property that could then be taken from the Native American Indians and sold to non-Indians. The Dawes Act really was not democratic, because the US Congress had written and passed it without Indian representation, for Indians were not US citizens and therefore were not allowed to vote. Let's face it: the Dawes Act was a law made about Indian people for Indian people without any Indian representation![32]

For Sophia, there wasn't much reservation land left to return to. Many Oneidas had moved in with their relatives to make ends meet, and most still supported themselves by farming. Sophia's parents were not living with each other at this time, so Sophia stayed with Elizabeth in Oneida. Nicholas, now remarried, was living in a third-floor flat in Appleton, Wisconsin.

This is how Salt Pork Avenue in looked 1902 when Elizabeth lived there. Sadly, Oneidas literally lived in shacks, as the reservation was very poor.

Figure 23-Salt Pork Avenue in 1902. Photo courtesy of Oneida Museum.

As the wagon headed toward Elizabeth's log house, she and Sophia and Nicholas talked Oneida to each other. I thank God—or our Creator, as we indigenous tribes here in America call the Lord—that Sophia had maintained her knowledge of the Oneida language and so was able to converse with her parents (who spoke only Oneida), even after all those years out east. I learned from relatives that Sophia had secretly practiced speaking Oneida while alone, and she may have participated in a group with other Oneidas on outings in New Jersey to practice their language. I know members of other tribes, such as the Navajo, who secretly met to maintain their languages. These Native Americans on outings had to be very careful not to be caught speaking their native tongues, because even outside Carlisle, Indian language was taboo. But Sophia was careful, and she never lost her knowledge of her native language.

Not all Native American Indians who attended Carlisle were as lucky. Some could only speak English when they returned to their reservations, so they could no longer communicate with their parents. This was tragic.

The wagon turned down a dirt driveway and headed toward a small log house. As Sophia got out, she was greeted by family members waiting to see her, including Lily! They ran toward each other and hugged and cried their eyes out. A small Oneida girl looked up at Sophia, whom she didn't recognize. The family introduced Sophia to her little sister, Mary. Sophia and Mary smiled at each other, greeted each other in Oneida, hugged, and cried.

Sophia spent this summer of 1902 getting reacquainted with family and friends. She was so happy to be home and with them. She cried and cried tears of happiness, and so did her family and friends. Sophia shared stories of everything that had happened to her during her year at Carlisle and about her life for the past ten years with Mary and Abel Tomlinson in New Jersey.

Family and friends gathered for a celebration to welcome Sophia back to Oneida. Sophia hadn't had fry bread and corn soup for years, and they tasted so good, especially because she was eating them with family and friends.

Sophia told her family that she would visit for two months before returning to her work in New Jersey as Carlisle and the Tomlinson's expected. I find it mind-boggling that she was supposed to return to her work as a servant in New Jersey after a short visit with her Oneida family and friends.

Sophia settled in and helped Elizabeth with chores around the house and planting crops, and she spent time just talking to her mother. Sophia learned that many on the reservation were very poor. Few people had jobs, and many couldn't find work off the reservation either because they were Native American Indians.

Sophia also caught up with Lily. She learned that Lily had returned to Oneida in the late 1890s and married a man named Josiah Baird. Later on, Lily and Josiah divorced. Lily fell in love with a man named John Stevens, and they made their living farming in Oneida. Lily also managed to find work in Green Bay, Wisconsin, and lived there for a time before returning to the Oneida Reservation. According to NARA records, Lily she had been on various outings from Carlisle, and Sophia was absolutely shocked to learn that Lily had only spent about three days at the Carlisle Indian Industrial Boarding School before being sent out to work as a servant in the countryside. So much for Carlisle educating Indians.

According to records from the Holy Apostles Episcopal Church, Lily, John Stevens, and their daughter, Josephine Stevens, are buried in unmarked graves in the church cemetery. Lily passed away in the early 1930s while living in Hobart, Wisconsin. I do not know what caused her death. Lily and John had other children together and lived most of their lives in Oneida and Hobart. I never got to meet Lily, my great-aunt, although I would've loved to have gotten to know her. I am grateful I was able to meet Sophia and learn about her.

One day in July 1902, Sophia was outdoors hanging laundry on the clothesline to dry when a young man walking down the road waved to her and yelled hello. Sophia looked up at him. He had dark brown hair and blue eyes. He waved and shouted hello again. Sophia shyly said hello and waved, not knowing she had a pair of underpants scrunched up in her hand. The man smiled at Sophia and approached the fence that bordered the yard to talk to her.

Grandma Millie's version of this story goes like this: "Sophia is hanging laundry. A young man waves and smiles at her and says hello. Sophia smiles back at him. She holds up a big pair of underpants and waves the underpants at the young man."

I laughed and laughed at this hysterical version, knowing fully that this was a bullshit version of the story of her parents' first meeting. Grandma Millie giggled too. She liked to BS with her grandchildren and other relatives. Like her mother, Sophia, Grandma Millie had a lot of feistiness and humor in her.

After greeting each other, Sophia and this man, Theodore Hyson Powless, whom everyone called Hyson, talked by the fence for a while. Hyson, my great-grandfather, had a nice, quick smile and *blue* eyes—a rare feature for a Native American Indian. Sophia was shy but enjoyed talking with him. She felt at ease with him. Hyson invited Sophia out on a date, and then he continued his walk down Salt Pork Avenue.

Figure 24-Here is an early photo of Theodore
Hyson Powless, my Great Grandfather.

Sophia's heart pounded and raced a mile a minute. Not realizing how much time she had spent at the fence talking to Hyson, she quickly resumed hanging the wet laundry on the clothesline. When she finished, she headed back inside the log house, thrilled she was going on a date with this young man.

Sophia and Hyson went on multiple dates that summer. She fell in love with him, and he with her. She was very happy. They learned much about each other on their dates.

Grandma Millie shared with me that her father, Hyson, was Oneida Indian born in Oneida, Wisconsin, in 1872. Like Sophia and Lily, he too was sent away to a boarding school out east to be assimilated into white culture. Hyson, his brothers Alfred and Richard, and his sister Abbey all attended the Hampton Institute in Hampton, Virginia, in the late 1880s and 1890s. Hyson's elder relatives were prominent chiefs or leaders in the Oneida tribe. Because of this, it was crucial that Hyson and his siblings be sent away to a boarding school to break the chain of Indian leadership and intimidate and control the elder Powless leaders. Of the four Powless siblings who attended Hampton, only Richard graduated, in 1888. Upon his graduation from Hampton Institute, Richard (like all graduates) was required to recite a pledge stating that he wanted to be "civilized" and to become a Christian missionary upon his return to the Oneida Reservation. Can you imagine the graduates stating that they wanted to be "civilized" and that were supposed to become Christian missionaries?[33] Well, Richard did not become a missionary. He had already been baptized as Episcopal as a child in Oneida, before he was sent to Hampton Institute, and he already was civilized, as were all Native American Indians in this country. He wasn't a wild savage. However, because he spoke Oneida and had been brought up in Oneida culture, the US government did not consider him civilized. The government wanted him to follow only white culture and to speak only English.

Richard was a very intelligent, hardworking man. When he left Hampton, he became a printer in the Boston area, and he worked as a teacher, farmer, and surveyor when he returned to Oneida.[34]

Hyson worked with Richard at Houghton-Mifflin Riverside Press in Cambridge, Massachusetts, beginning in February 1892 as part of his outing experience. By December, Hyson decided he did not want to return to Hampton Institute, so he stayed in the Boston area and worked as a printer at Riverside Press for five years. He wrote a letter to Hampton explaining why he was leaving the school. Hyson's handwriting was beautiful. The Hampton Institute had nothing but kind words to say about him, including that they loved his bright, cheery face and quick, pleasant smiles.

Figure 25-Here is a letter Hyson wrote to the
Hampton Institute, December, 1892.

In 1897, after working for Riverside Press and attending night school, Hyson decided he wanted to go back home to Oneida to settle down. I do not know what night classes he took in Boston, but I suspect that they focused on printing or making advertising signs. Back home in Oneida, Hyson looked for printing work, but there were no jobs in this trade on the reservation, and there were very few jobs available, period. So Hyson tried to find a printing job off the reservation. Sadly, because he was Native American Indian, no one would hire him, so he became a farmer on the reservation, helping his older brother Richard. Grandma Millie said Hyson also played in a band with his two brothers. His instrument was the trombone. Like Sophia, Hyson had also participated in outings. Records give the following timeline for this work:

1887: Sheffield, MA. Outing with Mrs. Bushness, earning fifteen dollars for three months' work.

1889: Onondaga Valley, NY. Outing. Five dollars for one month's work.

1890: Castle, NY. Outing with Mrs. Slocum, earning fifteen dollars for three months' work.

1892–1897: Riverside Press, Cambridge, MA. Outing, five years, printer.

Hyson was enrolled at Hampton for five and a half years, and he spent most of that time working on outings. He did not graduate from Hampton.

When Hyson met Sophia, he shared her love for music and dance, and they often went dancing.

That summer of 1902 seemed to go by very quickly, and Sophia soon realized she would have to board a train and return to New Jersey, where she was expected to work for Abel and Mary Tomlinson permanently. But things had changed for Sophia. She was now in love with Hyson and happier at home in Oneida with family and friends than she had been in years. Going with her heart and gut, Sophia decided to stay in Oneida permanently. This was a very difficult decision for her. She did love and respect Abel and Mary after working for them for ten years, but deep in her heart and soul, she knew she wanted to stay with Hyson and her family back home on the Oneida Reservation. She immediately let Abel and Mary know of her plans to not return to New Jersey. She did not tell Carlisle School of her plans. She didn't feel she had to contact them about what she wanted to do with her life.

Abel and Mary were beside themselves to hear of Sophia's decision and were determined to keep her as their servant. They reported Sophia decision to stay in Wisconsin to Carlisle Indian Industrial School's administration. Believe me; Carlisle was not happy to hear this news. Sophia was not playing by Carlisle's, the government or the Tomlinson's rules.

Abel took it upon himself to travel by train from his home in Laurel Springs, New Jersey, to Oneida, Wisconsin, to bring his top servant, Sophia, back with him. According to Uncle Gary and Grandma Millie, Abel tried like hell, wrangling and haggling, to get Sophia to come back east with him. The arguing went on for days. This was a very difficult time for Sophia and everyone else. She cried, Abel cried, everyone cried. This was heart-wrenching ordeal for all involved.

In the end, Abel returned back east without Sophia, who remained true to her feelings and her decision to stay in Oneida. She had not allowed the US government, Carlisle, or the Tomlinsons to dictate the course of her life. She did not want to continue being a servant to Abel and Mary in New Jersey. She wanted to be free to be herself, an Oneida Indian. She wanted to stay home on the Oneida Reservation with her Oneida tribe. And she did!

After learning that Sophia stayed in Oneida, I wondered whether Jemima Skenandore ever returned to New Jersey at the end of that summer. With the help of my friend Barb Skenandore, I was able to meet Jemima's son Walter, then eighty-six and still living in the house Jemima had lived in many years before. Walter was very kind and honest. He told me flat out that his mother had not returned to Carlisle or to New Jersey in 1902. He said, "No way would my mother have returned to Carlisle, Pennsylvania, or New Jersey to continue working as a servant ... She stayed home here in Oneida, where she wanted to live."

Records in the National Archives in Washington, DC, indicate that Jemima Skenandore was sent to Carlisle in August 1897. By April 1898, she was already sent out on an outing in Jenkintown, Pennsylvania. She didn't spend much time at Carlisle Indian Industrial Boarding School to become educated and civilized. Carlisle's records report that Jemima left school in June of 1902 because of expiration of time and again in November 1903 at her own request. These records were falsified by the Carlisle staff. There is no way that Carlisle would have let a student leave her own request. I'm sure Jemima's son Walter told the truth when he told me his mother had remained permanently in Oneida beginning in the summer of 1902.

Carlisle was not pleased to hear that Sophia did not return to the Tomlinsons' home, and the staff was not pleased that Jemima did not return to her outing in New Jersey either. Since the school's ultimate goal was the assimilation of Native American Indians into the white Euro-American culture, they would've preferred for Sophia and Jemima to live permanently as servants to white people on the East Coast. To Carlisle, Sophia's and Jemima's permanent return to the Oneida Reservation meant that "they had gone back to the blanket"—they had returned to their reservations and thus had failed to assimilate into white culture. Carlisle kept the money they had sent back from their jobs as punishment for their choosing to stay in Oneida.

After Abel left Wisconsin, Sophia and Hyson continued courting. By late fall 1902, Hyson proposed to Sophia. They were very happy and in love. They set their wedding date for late January 1903.

In November of 1902, Nicholas fell off a ladder at his home in Appleton, Wisconsin. Our family story is that Nicholas was doing some work on the roof of his home at the time. The real story, as published in The Oshkosh newspaper *The Daily Northwestern* on November 19, 1902 told the real story of this incident.

INDIAN'S SHOCKING FATE.

Breaks Leg and Suffers Three Amputations of the Member.

(Special to The Northwestern)

Appleton, Wis., Nov. 18.—While in an intoxicated condition at his home recently, Nicholas Huff, an Oneida Indian, was the victim of one of the most terrible accidents ever recorded among the tribe. While drunk, he proceeded to climb the ladder to the upper floor of his hut, where his sleeping apartment was located. He lost his grip on the rounds and fell backwards, catching his leg between the rounds and the wall.

The weight of his body was so great as to break the large bone in his leg, pressing the lower end of it through the flesh. He dropped to the floor and the exposed end of the bone landed onto the pine floor in such a manner and with such force as to make a deep depression in the wood. Here the unfortunate man lay in filth and squalor until nearly midnight, when some members of his family returned home and discovered his almost lifeless body. Huff had lost such a great quantity of strength and blood that it was almost impossible to revive him. The lower portion of the leg, however, was amputated and the man lived for several weeks. Blood poisoning finally set in and another amputation was necessary. A third amputation was finally necessary, the effects of which he could not withstand.

The attending physician this morning presented his bill for services before the county board of supervisors of Outagamie county, and the matter will be referred to the supreme court, as the local members of the board are of the opinion that the county board cannot be held liable for the debts thus incurred by the Oneida Indian.

Figure 26-Newspaper article reporting Nicholas Huff's accident.

As the article states, Nicholas never recovered from his leg injury, having had three surgeries on it. His last surgery was too much for him to take, and he passed away in early January 1903. His family mourned his passing. Sophia was devastated to lose her father just months after reuniting with him.

Sophia and Hyson continued with their plans and married on January 26, 1903, at the Holy Apostles Episcopal Church where Sophia had been baptized as an infant. After the wedding, they moved in with Hyson's brother because they were so poor. To support themselves, Hyson helped his brother on the farm, and Sophia worked as a cleaning lady for white people in the area.

Sophia And Hyson: The Early Years, 1903 to 1921

For years Sophia and Hyson continued living at Richard's farmhouse. Grandma Millie said they attended the Holy Apostles Episcopal Church in Oneida on Sundays and also participated in the church's social functions, such as potluck dinners and picnics. Sophia continued cleaning homes for white people in the area to earn money. To me, it seemed that she had picked up where she'd left off—she went from domestic training at Carlisle Indian Industrial Boarding School to working as a servant in New Jersey to cleaning homes for whites in Oneida. Sophia and Hyson continued going out to dances for entertainment, and Hyson also continued playing in the family band with his two brothers.

In April 1904, Sophia gave birth to their first child, a son named Henry, in Richard's home with the help of a midwife. Grandma Millie told me that all women on the reservation had their babies at home with midwives, for they could not afford to have their babies in hospitals. Sophia and Hyson were thrilled to have Henry. Then on June 6, 1906, Mildred Henrietta Powless—Grandma Millie—was born. Her parents gave her the Oneida Ka Na Lat, pronounced "GUN-ah-luck". She said that she couldn't remember what this meant, but I wasn't sure whether she really didn't know or whether she was afraid to tell me the meaning. Why? Grandma Millie spent most of her life in fear of the U.S. Government for maintaining her Oneida heritage.

I traveled to Oneida, Wisconsin to talk to the Oneida Language Staff on the reservation to see if they knew what Ka Na Lat meant in English, and they said it meant "Surprise." I laughed. This was a fitting name for Grandma Millie because she was feisty like her mother, and her humorous comments about life were always a surprise.

Grandma Millie's sister, Martina, was born in 1908, and Richard's log house was now crowded. Sophia and Hyson loved their children and were very happy, but they realized that they had to find a bigger place to settle down and raise their kids.

Around 1911 Sophia sold her allotted land, and she and Hyson used the money to build a home on Hyson's allotted land, which was right next door to Richard's log house and farmland. A 1917 map that shows Hyson's land on the corner of Osborne Road, right next to Richard's land. The area was then known as Osborne Town, next to Seymour, Wisconsin.[35]

Figure 27-1917 map of Osborne Road, Oneida
Reservation. Photo courtesy Ancestry.com.

Hyson wanted to live close to Richard so he could continue helping on the farm. Hyson and Sophia decided to enroll their three oldest children, Henry, Millie, and Martina, in the nearby Oneida Indian Boarding School for the 1911 to 1912 school year. I wondered why Sophia put her three kids in a boarding school when she herself had had such an unpleasant experience at the Carlisle Indian Industrial Boarding School. Grandma Millie told me that her mother was hesitant in enrolling her three children in the Oneida Boarding School, but had decided to do so to keep Millie, Martina, and Henry in a safe place while their new home was being built. This would give the kids a roof over their heads, a warm place to sleep, schooling, and meals in a place close enough that Sophia could check up on them. Thus, this school was unlike Carlisle, which didn't allow parents to see their kids for years. Sophia did visit to check up on her children on weekends and often on weekdays, too.

When Millie, Martina, and Henry left for the Oneida Indian Boarding School, Sophia made sure they had clean clothes with them and that they were clean and healthy. She had trimmed Henry's hair and had combed her daughters' long hair and styled it with pretty ribbons. The three children wore new, sewn outfits made by Sophia when they entered the Oneida Indian Boarding School.

Figure 28-Picture of Sophia's three eldest children: Mildred is standing on the left, Henry is sitting in the middle and Martina is standing at the right. Photo courtesy of Mildred H. Elm

Grandma Millie told me that one time when Sophia came to visit, Sophia was shocked to find that all three kids had caught head lice. She was furious! She went straight to the school administrator and said, "I brought my three kids here clean and scrubbed! I come here to visit them today and find all three of them have head lice! I will be back next weekend to visit my three children. They better not have one louse on them!" The next weekend when Sophia came back to visit, Henry, Martina, and Millie were clean and free of lice.

After a year had passed, the Powless home was complete. Sophia and Hyson took their children out of the boarding school and moved into their new home on Osborn Road. Hyson continued farming to support his family, and Sophia continued cleaning homes for non-Indians living nearby and taking care of her growing family and new home.

By 1920, Sophia and Hyson had had ten children, two of whom died in infancy and were buried in unmarked graves in the Holy Apostles Episcopal Church cemetery. Sophia and Hyson had chosen not to mark the graves so that their children's resting sites would not be disturbed. I do not know how these two babies died, but their death was heartbreaking for Sophia, Hyson, and the rest of their family. Sophia and Hyson secured burial sites near their deceased babies' graves so they would be reunited when they passed away. Only the immediate family knew where the two babies were buried.

Sophia was always a very hard worker. She wore many hats as a wife and mother and cleaning lady. She did her best to raise her eight surviving children. The family was poor, and everyone worked hard to survive on the reservation.

I've asked relatives many questions about Sophia and learned that besides working as a cleaning lady, she also picked string beans in the summers in nearby white farmers' fields for a wage of four cents per pound picked. If the children helped her, as they did when they got older, they earned a penny a pound apiece. All of these beans went to a nearby cannery. Grandma Millie said that the kids hated picking beans but did so to help sustain the family. Sophia did allow the children to use some of their bean-picking money to attend the Seymour Fair each summer. All of the kids would pile into a horse-drawn wagon with Sophia and Hyson. Everyone looked forward to the fair, and Grandma Millie said that the prospect of going made picking beans not so bad. They were rewarded with some play after all their back-breaking work. The kids relished these summer outings.

Sophia loved to garden and was very good at it, according to Grandma Millie and other relatives. To help feed her family, she grew berries, corn, cabbage, cucumbers, beets, and other vegetables, and she sold some of the berries she grew. She also grew beautiful flowers. Her favorite flowers were gladiolas, and I think of Great-Grandma

Sophie every time I see them. I wish I had Sophia's green thumb and her thoughtfulness for plants, but as my husband says, I'm a "plant murderess" because I either forget or get too lazy to water any plants we have. Grandma Millie told me that Sophia used to sell some of her flowers to a local bar for spending money.

Figure 29-Sophia picking her homegrown berries.

Grandma Millie also said that her mother used to get up very early each morning to milk a cow her family owned. Sophia would then go quickly to a nearby factory to sell the milk. She had to rush because this factory had a deadline each morning for when milk could be brought in to be processed, and Sophia's family needed the milk money.

One time when Sophia was helping Hyson plow a field on their farm, it suddenly started pouring rain. Puddles quickly formed in the field. When it stopped raining, Hyson wanted to quit for the day to allow the puddles to dry up before continuing to plow, but Sophia would have none of this quitting! She took the plow and pushed it herself, spraying mud and water all over herself and Hyson and anyone else who happened to be standing nearby. Despite being soaking wet and muddy, Sophia continued to plow that field, until the job was done.

Grandma Millie mentioned that when Sophia had to go clean someone's house, relatives pitched in to take care of the kids. The Oneidas used the term "working out" to refer to an Oneida woman's work cleaning a non-Indian's house.

Sophia did not have any favorites among her eight children and treated them all equally. They all did chores around the house and farm daily, and they all attended school and church. Sophia did not teach her kids much of the Oneida language for fear of retribution from the US government, and my uncle Richard told me that Oneidas were afraid to share their native culture and language with their children when he was a child.

Around 1914 Sophia wanted to visit Mary and Abel Tomlinson in Laurel Springs, New Jersey. I was shocked to learn about this from Grandma Millie and other relatives, but it was true. She talked this over with Hyson. They decided that she would take a train out east along with two of their children. Grandma Millie, who was then seven, and her little sister Cordelia, who was just an infant, went along with Sophia. Hyson paid for this trip. He and other relatives took care of the other children left at home in Oneida.

When Sophia, Millie, and Cordelia boarded the train, they brought food for the three-day trip and enough clothes for their stay. Millie and Cordelia had never been on a train before. As Millie watched out the train windows, everything outside seemed so big to her since she was just a little girl. She sat quietly by Sophia and just took in the countryside as they traveled.

Abel and Mary were excited for Sophia and her daughters' visit. It had been twelve years since they had last seen Sophia. Abel and Mary met Sophia and the girls at the Rancocas/Laurel Springs Train Depot, and Sophia greeted them in English, hugged them, and introduced Millie and Cordelia. Grandma Millie told me that everyone at the depot stared at Cordelia, as they had never seen an Indian baby before, and smiled at Millie. They also were very curious about the cradle board that Sophia carried Cordelia in, for they had never seen one of these either.

Abel and Mary helped Sophia and the girls into the wagon, and they all headed to the Tomlinson's redbrick home. Sophia talked to Abel and Mary as the horse galloped on. Grandma Millie said the area was beautiful. Sophia visited with relatives of Abel and Mary and old friends in the area and friends in Maryland during their approximately six-month stay. During this time, Millie attended the "school on the hill" that had been built long before by Abel's relative Ephraim Tomlinson. Sophia did not visit the Carlisle Indian Industrial Boarding School, according to Grandma Millie and the Carlisle School Visitor Book at NARA.

Sophia did not visit Carlisle, for she had been mistreated and abused by staff when she was in attendance from 1891 to 1892. Therefore, as Grandma Millie said, Sophia had no reason to visit.

I have read accounts of former Carlisle students who enjoyed their time there and fondly called it "Dear Old Carlisle." However, some of students used this nickname even if they didn't have a good experience at the school, thus sugarcoating their negative experiences. I've also read other accounts of Carlisle students who did not have fond memories of the school. Memories of Carlisle were not very pleasant for Sophia. School staff was strict, even mentally and physically abusive. I cannot document these incidents, but Sophia told stories of her mistreatment at the school to Grandma Millie and other relatives. Of the approximately 10,000 Native American Indian children from across this country who attended Carlisle between 1879 and 1918, only approximately 760 actually graduated. About 192 children are buried in the tiny school cemetery, but many more children are believed to have died at this school or on outings and were never heard from or seen again. One of these children was a relative of mine. To Sophia, Carlisle was not "Dear Old Carlisle."

At Abel and Mary Tomlinson's home, Sophia, Millie, and Cordelia slept in a bedroom above a side porch that had been a summer kitchen when Sophia had worked as a servant there. Grandma Millie said that the bedroom was big enough for the three of them and that when it got cold, a woodstove heated the room. The stable that had been next to the summer kitchen had since been torn down.

Millie played with Abel and Mary's niece and other the local children. Sophia showed Millie around the home and grounds. Millie loved the nearby lake. Sophia hadn't attended school during her a time as a servant.

Sophia got reacquainted with the house she had lived in for ten years. The tiny bedrooms were still there in the middle of the house on the second floor. Sophia remembered sleeping in all of them over the years. She took Millie up the narrow, steep servants' stairs. Millie felt like she was climbing a steep mountain. Grandma Millie told me that Sophia slept in the big room above the screened porch during her ten years working for Abel and Mary, but this isn't true, as that room wasn't there until after Sophia had returned to Oneida in 1902. I don't know whether Sophia told Grandma Millie about where she really slept, but I suspect she did. Perhaps Grandma Millie had tried to sugarcoat the information she told me about her mother's stay by saying that Sophia slept in this big room rather than one of the tiny servants' bedrooms in the middle of the second floor.

I am glad Sophia and her daughters visited the Tomlinson's and that Sophia, Abel, and Mary were able to get reacquainted and restore their friendship.

After six months had gone by, Sophia and the two girls traveled, by train, back to Oneida, Wisconsin. They'd had a wonderful visit with

Abel and Mary. Grandma Millie shared with me that Abel and Mary gave Sophia a colt as a present. Sophia was surprised and touched to receive this horse, which she loaded onto the train to bring back to Oneida with her.

Sophia and the Tomlinson's respected each other, and Sophia kept in touch with them through letters after this visit. Sophia's experience serving the Tomlinson's for ten years had taught her and them much. Yes, she had been a servant, but Mary and Abel had grown to respect and even love her and vice versa. If Carlisle had had their way, Sophia would have lived out her life as the Tomlinson's' servant—ultimately becoming completely assimilated into white culture. My research told me that Sophia earned the position of head servant in the Tomlinson household, in charge of all the other servants, and thus her leadership, strong work ethic, and loyalty were very valuable to Abel and Mary. Their warm welcome of Sophia back into their home and their gift of a colt showed their love for Sophia, as my Uncle Gary told me they did. And Sophia did love them.

As Sophia, Millie, Cordelia, and the colt headed back to Wisconsin, Sophia listened to the train's engine chug west. Sophia was happy that she had visited Abel and Mary and rekindled her friendship with them, and she was proud to have introduced Millie and Cordelia to them. The Tomlinson's were equally happy that Sophia and her daughters had visited.

After another three-day train ride, Sophia, the girls, and the colt finally arrived in Oneida, tired but happy to be home. Hyson and the rest of the family came to the Oneida Depot to greet them. Hyson was glad Sophia and the girls had had a good visit out east, and he was in awe to see a colt arrive with them. He very much appreciated this gift, and the family took good care of it. Abel had thoughtfully paid for the colt's transportation to Wisconsin.

Sophia cried and hugged her other children and Hyson, as she hadn't seen them for months.

The family grew over the years. Sophia and Hyson continued running their farm the best they could. Sophia sewed all the clothes for the family, as they were too poor to buy clothes at stores, and she also washed all the family's laundry by hand in a bucket with a washboard. She taught all of her daughters to sew on a treadle machine. Grandma Millie told me that this skill proved useful later in life, as she supported herself and her family by sewing in a factory in downtown Milwaukee for thirty years.

Grandma Millie said that Sophia and Hyson loved music and dancing. Somehow, Hyson was able to obtain a used Victrola, and he played songs on it and taught all the kids to dance. Grandma Millie was a fantastic dancer and loved to dance, like her parents. Sophia and Hyson went out dancing and to the bars on Saturday nights. Relatives babysat the children on these nights. Hyson also continued in the band with his brothers.

During this time, women were not allowed to drink in bars. They had to wait in an adjoining room, called a sitting room, while the men drank in the barroom. Hyson did drink, and Grandma Millie and other relatives told me that he was known as a party boy. Sophia did not drink at all then. Oneida Indians did not frequent bars that non-Indians did, and the two groups interacted only when the Oneidas were working for non-Indians.

Sophia and Hyson's children attended school in Osborne Town near Seymour, and they all learned English and spoke Oneida very little for fear of retribution from the US government. I find it so sad that my relatives weren't taught their language, and I find it repulsive that anything related to their culture was taboo. It angers me that our ancestors lived in fear of sharing their language and culture with the next generation.

I asked Grandma Millie about her grandmother, Elizabeth Huff, whom she and her siblings called Grandma Huff. I learned that when Elizabeth visited, she usually walked the couple of miles from her log house on Salt Pork Avenue to Sophia and Hyson's farm on Osborne Road. Grandma Millie and her brothers and sisters would look out the window and see Grandma Huff in the distance walking down a hill toward their farm and shout, "Here comes Grandma Huff!" Millie and the rest of the kids would then greet her with hugs at the door. Sophia then greeted her mother at the door and spoke with her in Oneida. None of Sophia's kids could speak Oneida, so they could not talk to Grandma Huff or understand her conversations with Sophia, but they sat nearby and listened to these conversations. Bored, they eventually left the two women alone and went elsewhere. Grandma Millie said this was because "Well, I couldn't understand Grandma Huff because she only spoke Oneida. Me and my brothers and sisters just left the room because we could not speak to Grandma Huff anyway."

When Grandma Millie told me this, my heart sank. If the US government had allowed Oneida children to learn and speak their own language, Grandma Millie and her siblings would've been able to communicate with Elizabeth and would've gotten to know her. I think Elizabeth would've been receptive to learning English if she were allowed to continue speaking her native language. Then Millie and her siblings could have joined in Elizabeth and Sophia's conversations. Elizabeth watched her grandkids leave the room many times when she wanted them to stay and spend time with her. Can you imagine how Elizabeth felt when her grandchildren left soon after she arrived? She never got to know her grandchildren. Sophia was an interpreter of sorts, being able to speak both languages, but these children should have been able to learn both Oneida and English.

It was sad that it was forbidden for these children to be who they were simply because the US government said so. I can't help but think of what a former student at the Carlisle Indian Industrial Boarding School, Luther Standing Bear, said years after he had left Carlisle:

> So, we went to school to copy, to imitate, not to exchange languages and ideas, and not to develop the best traits that had come out of unaccountable experiences of hundreds of thousands of years living on this continent. So, while the white people had much to teach us, we had much to teach them, and what a school could have been established upon that ideal. [36]

Luther Standing Bear had such insight. His words are so true.

Unfortunately, some Native American Indian children who did attend boarding schools like Carlisle to learn to be white fully lost their Indian language and came home to their reservations unable to speak them. Bill Wright, a Pattwin Indian sent to Steward Indian School in Nevada at six years old, returned to his reservation years later unable to speak the Pattwin language with his relatives. In 1945 Bill's grandmother spoke Pattwin to him, but he couldn't understand her. A relative nearby interpreted her words: she wanted Bill to speak Pattwin with her. He told her in English, "Grandma, I don't understand you." She then said to Bill in Pattwin, "Then who are you?" Bill cried and cried. When I heard Bill talk about this on the video *Our Spirits Don't Speak English*, I cried too. Bill vowed right there and then to relearn Pattwin. And he did.[37]

After Sophia and Elizabeth finished their conversations in Oneida, Elizabeth would head out the door and walk the couple of miles back to her home. Grandma Millie and her siblings loved and respected Grandma Huff, but the language barrier kept them from really getting to know each other as family.

By 1920, Sophia had given birth to her last child, a son named Lloyd. World War I was now over, and conditions were still bleak on the reservation. Sophia and Hyson were still very poor, and although they did their best to provide for their children, survival was really a day-to-day struggle.

The Burke Act, which passed Congress in 1906, sped up the process of turning properties owned by the Oneidas and other Native American Indians over to white owners. This act was one of the most racist laws to ever come out of Washington, DC. It allowed the secretary of the interior to determine if an Indian individual was competent enough to own property. Many Indians across this country had received titles to their land but knew nothing of paying taxes, mortgages, or fraud, so because of the Burke Act, they lost their lands and homes. Sophia and Hyson were able to keep their farm during this time, and they worked hard to take care of it and their children.

The Middle Years: 1922 to 1942

Around 1922, Grandma Millie, then a sixteen-year-old teenager, moved with Sophia to Green Bay so Millie could attend Green Bay West High School. Hyson stayed on the farm in Oneida, and some of the children were sent to live with other relatives to make ends meet. Grandma Millie said that her mother and Hyson often separated around this time. Hyson had a tendency to party and could be lazy, and I'm sure this contributed to the separations. When Sophia and Millie arrived in Green Bay, they stayed with Sophia's sister Lily, and Sophia found a job as a cleaning lady and maid in a downtown Green Bay hotel. She and Millie woke up every day around 3:00 a. m. Millie helped her mother clean at the hotel, scrubbing a marble staircase there every morning while Sophia cleaned in another part of the hotel. After a few hours, they headed to the hotel kitchen to scrounge around for food to eat for their breakfast. Then Millie would get ready and head to the high school. and Sophia would continue her cleaning work.

Millie was one of few Native American Indians attending Green Bay West High School at this time. One time when Millie was walking home from school, she saw that a barbershop was open. She had wanted to have her long black hair cut short for quite a while, so she walked up to the shop and slowly opened the door. As she entered, she asked the barber, "Would you please cut my hair short? I can pay you for this."

The barber looked at her beautiful long black hair and said, "Are you sure you want me to cut your hair? I'm a barber, not a beautician."

Millie looked him straight in the eye and said, "Well, I don't care if you are a barber. Would you please cut my hair short for me?"

The barber said, "Okay." He told Millie to sit down in the chair and proceeded to cut her hair short. Millie watched in the mirror as her long black locks fell to the floor. When the barber had finished, Millie paid him, thanked him, and left.

Millie couldn't wait to show Sophia her new hairdo. When Sophia met Millie at the door, she gasped at the sight of her daughter's hair and burst into tears. Grandma Millie said she cried for hours. She hadn't wanted Millie to cut her hair short because in Oneida tradition, women didn't cut their hair unless they were in mourning. Sophia never cut her own hair, and her long hair was part of her heritage. To Sophia, Millie's short haircut was a sign that she had assimilated into white society. Millie really didn't understand the meaning of this Oneida custom, and because the government frowned upon the sharing of Indian culture with children, I'm sure Sophia did not go into detail about it. Grandma Millie was badly mistreated at the high school because of her Oneida heritage and called savage, squaw, and many other derogatory names. I have the feeling that Millie had cut her hair to fit in with the other non-Indian students.

By 1923, a year after she had come to Green Bay, Millie wrote a letter to her father, who was now living in Milwaukee with relatives and working in a factory, explaining that she was unhappy in Green Bay and wanted to come live with him in Milwaukee. She said she was constantly teased at school and was struggling to get good grades because, with one exception, none of her teachers would help her. Dismayed, she wanted to get away from the prejudice she faced. Sophia and Hyson allowed Millie to leave Green Bay and to live in Milwaukee. Millie left one semester short of graduating high school.

Sophia stayed on in Green Bay for a few months, continuing her work at the hotel, before joining Millie and Hyson in Milwaukee. Sophia and Millie found work as laundry ladies at Deaconess Hospital in downtown Milwaukee, where Millie's sister Martina already worked as a hospital messenger, delivering mail and newspapers to patients. She also did orderly work, watered plants, and tidied up patients' rooms. The rest of Sophia and Hyson's children were scattered in homes of other relatives. Besides doing hospital laundry, Sophia also continued cleaning homes for non-Indians in the Milwaukee area.

Hyson and Sophia still owned their farm in Oneida, and Richard took care of it along with his own farm. Eventually, Sophia and Hyson returned to the farm. Their children were now older, and some of them were married. Sophia and Hyson took care of the grandchildren on their farm during the summer. Though poor, they managed to survive on proceeds from farming and odd jobs, including Sophia's cleaning work, which she did her entire life.

When the Depression struck the country in 1929, the Oneida Reservation got even poorer. Jobs became even scarcer, as they did throughout the country. Grandma Millie said that the US government gave food rations to the Oneidas. Many families once again banded together under one roof to survive. Sanitary conditions were very poor; as there were not many homes on the reservation with indoor plumbing.[38] Grandma Millie said that most of the homes were rundown shacks. There was a lot of despair and hopelessness for the Oneida at this time. Grandma Millie said there were a lot of bars in the area, and my research confirms that in 1930, Oneida had fifteen taverns. By 1939 approximately 1,300 of the 1,500 Oneidas living on the reservation were receiving government aid in the form of surplus commodities, WPA assistance, outdoor relief, old-age pensions, dependent-children pension, or CCC aid. Sophia, Hyson, and their relatives managed to get by.[39]

In 1941, the United States entered World War II. Adolf Hitler was in charge in Germany, and his army was murdering Jewish people and people of other nationalities. Prior to the war, he commented on how much he liked the way the US government had set up Indian reservations here in America. He set up his concentration camps much like our reservations. Prisoners in these camps were not allowed to leave. Since Indians were not allowed to be US citizens until 1924, the government held control over their land and them, treating them as though they were not able to take care of themselves and demonizing Indian culture. Even after gaining citizenship in 1924, the government still continued controlling Indians lives and their lands.

Hitler's plan to eradicate Jews and others in concentration camps was the Holocaust. Here in America, Native American Indians were also killed in a holocaust. We weren't put into gas chambers, but the US government tried to kill the Indian in us, heart and soul, by forbidding our culture and language. Indian children were forcefully taken from their families and sent far away to boarding schools to become assimilated into white society. Tribes were forced to move off their tribal lands and onto reservations, where they were dependents of the US government. These reservations were usually on poor lands, and thus Indians lived in perpetual poverty, dependent on the government for rations and just about everything else they needed to survive.

American history classes don't mention much about the Native American holocaust that happened right here in the good old United States of America. Not only have Indians been stereotyped on television and in movies, but true facts about Indian lands being taken away and given to non-Indians has been kept out of the history books. Not many people know why the Carlisle Indian Industrial Boarding School was set up and what it was really for. I didn't, and I was shocked when I found out that it and many other boarding schools here in the United States were a government experiment for "killing the Indian" by assimilating us into white culture.

In February 1941, Elizabeth Hill Huff Denny passed away. This was a very sad time for Sophia, who was very close to her mother and loved her mother dearly. Elizabeth had taught Sophia a lot and had been a good mother to Sophia and her siblings. Elizabeth was buried in the Holy Apostles Episcopal Church cemetery, and Sophia visited her mother's grave often to pay her respects.

On January 10, 1942, Richard Solatice Powless, Hyson's older brother, also passed away. Richard had lived most of his life in Oneida. Grandma Millie said that his wake was held in his log house on his farm, following Oneida custom. She mentioned that some of the older female relatives got together and removed a divider wall inside the log house to make room for all the mourners who came to pay their last respects to Richard. This wake lasted about three days, with many people coming and going. Mourners took turns sitting in a circle of chairs surrounding Richard's body. Food that Richard liked was served. Everyone pitched in to help with this funeral, even bringing food to the gathering. Richard was also buried in the Holy Apostles Episcopal Church cemetery. Hyson was sad about Richard's passing, as he looked up to his older brother and loved and respected him.

After Richard's death, Sophia and Hyson stayed on at their own farm and tried very hard to survive, but the Depression and World War II had taken its toll on the Oneida Reservation, as it had on the whole country. Sophia and Hyson couldn't keep up with their farm's finances, and in 1942, they sold the farm and move back to Milwaukee to live with relatives. Hyson took whatever work he could find in the city, whether it was painting signs, printing, or factory work. The Powless children were now all adults and on their own. Some had also moved to Milwaukee and others had moved to Chicago and other big cities to make a living. There just wasn't enough work available on the reservation. Sophia continued to do what she had been doing for most of her life: clean homes for non-Indians. She and Hyson stayed in Milwaukee for the next four or five years, living with one relative or another, continuing the lifestyle pattern they followed their entire lives. Like them, many Native American Indians lived only for survival, paycheck to paycheck, if they even had jobs at all.

Figure 30-1938 photo of Sophia and Hyson on their farm in Oneida, WI.

The Later Years: 1943 to 1964

World War II ended in 1945, and afterward, Sophia and Hyson really missed Oneida, so they moved back in the late 1940s. Since the war was now over, they figured their job prospects in Oneida would have improved. Because they had sold their farm years before, they rented a home on the reservation. Again Sophia found work as a cleaning lady. Hyson did any odd jobs he could find, including printing work. Grandma Millie said that he worked for white farmers in the area. Sophia and Hyson also helped their adult children by caring for grandchildren in the summers or even year round. The Oneida Reservation was still very poor. It would take several more decades for the Oneida to recover from the effects of the Dawes Act of 1879, the Burke Act of 1906, World War I, the Great Depression, and World War II. Unemployment and poverty were abundant, and as a result, Oneidas felt hopelessness and despair once again. This led some Indians into alcohol abuse.

By the 1950s, Sophia and Hyson were once again struggling, so they headed back to Milwaukee. Grandma Millie told me that her parents rotated among relatives houses. Now that Sophia and Hyson were getting up in years, finding employment was even more difficult. Sophia resorted to her old standby job as a cleaning lady, but Hyson's health was failing, so he couldn't work. He suffered from dementia, and

Grandma Millie said he had to be monitored at all times by relatives and by Sophia when she wasn't working. He was also very hard of hearing. He and Sophia lived off whatever money she earned cleaning homes and a monthly social security check, which usually came in the mail around the first of the month. Sophia tried to get home quickly from her cleaning job on that day so she could get the check from the mailbox before Hyson could. If Hyson got it first, he would go to the nearest bar, cash it, and proceed to drink. This behavior greatly angered Sophia because she and Hyson needed that money to live.

One day in June of 1954, Hyson felt very ill. Sophia was out cleaning someone's house, and the other relatives were also out working, so Hyson was home alone. At that time, my father, Bob, a policeman in Milwaukee, just happened to stop by for a visit and found Hyson so ill that he called an ambulance.

Hyson had suffered a heart attack, and he passed away at the hospital.

Sophia came home from her cleaning job to find out that Hyson had died. Beset with grief, she decided it best to take her husband's body back to Oneida for funeral services and burial in the Holy Apostles Episcopal Church cemetery, for she knew that that was what he would have wanted.

After Hyson's funeral, Sophia returned to Milwaukee and continued living with relatives and cleaning homes. In her spare time, she visited relatives, grandchildren, and great-grandchildren, many of whom lived in the Milwaukee area. Grandma Millie and other relatives drove her to these visits.

Figure 31-Photo of Sophia and Hyson taken in the 1950s

Some of my relatives have told me that Sophia loved to go to John's Bar and Swedes Bar in Milwaukee. She wore a little black hat and always carried a little black purse for these outings. At this time she suffered from asthma, so she kept a small bottle of blackberry brandy in that purse. I believe my relatives when they say that she used it only for medicinal purposes, as she certainly didn't drink much alcohol.

Sophia, being feisty, spoke her mind, but she was fair and honest when she spoke. She never stopped working, and she was cleaning non-Indian homes up to the day she suffered a heart attack in her late eighties. On February 4, 1965, after having a heart attack, Sophia passed away in a local hospital.

Grandma Millie told me that *everyone* was devastated to learn of Sophia's passing. It just didn't seem possible for her to die, as she had so much energy, spunk, and life in her!

My story has now come full circle to the time when I was around seven years old, in the early 1960s. I think back to when I first met Great-Grandma Sophie and to when I first saw the photo on display in the Milwaukee Public Museum of a woman I didn't know was my great-great-grandmother Elizabeth Huff. I have learned that these two women worked very hard during their lifetimes. So why have I shared these stories of Elizabeth and Sophia's lives with you?

When I learned that the old woman in the museum photo was related to me and that Sophia had attended Carlisle for a year and worked as a servant for another ten years, I knew I would learn a few things about their lives. I have since learned so much more than that. I have come to learn about myself and my Oneida heritage—a heritage I never really knew anything about! Through my research, I learned why I didn't know about it. For Grandma Millie's generation, passing along information about Oneida culture and language, or the culture and language of any Native American Indian tribe, was taboo. Today, I wish I hadn't been so shy or afraid to ask Sophia questions when she was still alive. Then again, I was only seven and she was in her eighties when we first met. What questions does a seven-year-old know to ask an elder relative about her family's culture, especially when that seven-year-old has no clue what her family's culture even is? Today, in my sixties, I have the wisdom to ask such questions. How I wish I had the wisdom I have today when I was a child.

Life doesn't work that way, however. This reminds me of Joni Mitchell's song "Big Yellow Taxi," which includes the line, "Don't it always seem to go that you don't know what you've got till it's gone."

I realized this as I researched Sophia's life story from 2000 to 2013. Never had I expected that I'd be researching and traveling for thirteen years, let alone writing a story to share with you about these two ladies and myself. Yes, Sophia and Elizabeth are long gone, but their spirits live on in me. I love singing around the house, and I'm sure I got my singing voice from Sophia. I have run marathons and like to walk, which I probably received from Elizabeth. For years and years I looked Indian on the outside but didn't feel Indian on the inside. Today, I know about my Oneida Indian heritage thanks to what I've learned about Sophia and Elizabeth. I look like Sophia and Elizabeth, and now I know why! I am now proud to know just who I really am.

After Sophia passed away, my older siblings and I were allowed to attend her wake in Milwaukee. I don't remember where it was held, but I remember walking into a dimly lit room, where she was laid out in her casket for viewing. Candles burned in the room, and many relatives and friends, mostly women, sat in a semicircle before Sophia, who was wearing her traditional dark clothing and had her long hair up in its usual bun. It was tradition for ladies to sit in a circle around the body of the deceased. I had never seen this before Sophia's wake.

The room was very quiet as I prayed next to Sophia's open coffin and paid my last respects to her. Then my siblings and I left the room and headed back home. Because I had nine siblings at this time, my immediate family did not make the long trip to Oneida and Holy Apostles Episcopal Church for Sophia's burial. On a very cold, snowy day in February 1965, she was interred in the cemetery next to Hyson. Relatives tell me that it was a very sad day for everyone who knew Sophia. The cemetery is hilly, so it was very difficult for some of the elderly Oneidas to climb through the snow to Sophia's final resting place, but everyone helped each other to make the journey to pay their final respects at Sophia's gravesite.

Everyone who knew Sophia loved and respected her. Grandma Millie told me that after the funeral, everyone went to a local bar for a drink, which is ironic, as Sophia didn't have her first drink until she was in her fifties and barely drank after that.

My relative Winnifred "Honey-Bunny" Rosalez shared the following story about Sophia: One evening Sophia went to a bar in Milwaukee with some family members. Patrons at this bar all knew her and loved her so much that they each bought her a drink. Sophia, being very tiny and not much of a drinker, knew she couldn't drink all those drinks, so she poured the drinks into a potted plant behind her seat when people weren't looking. That plant got plenty of water that night! My relative joked that the plant either grew really tall, straight through the bar's ceiling, or keeled over in a drunken stupor from all the firewater Sophia poured into it!

Sophia and her mother, Elizabeth, were never famous. They were just two people trying to live their lives. I see them as very strong women. Their story is really no different than those of many American people of many ethnicities. Sophia and Elizabeth overcame the degradation Native American Indians faced from the US government and non-Indians by maintaining their Oneida heritage and language. As I share their stories with you, I share a part of myself that I didn't know about for years: my Oneida Indian heritage.

No, I cannot speak Oneida. No, I cannot read Oneida. No, I don't know much about the Oneida people. But because I've learned about Elizabeth and Sophia through my research, I have learned not to be ashamed to be an Oneida Indian. I admire these two ladies for their perseverance in preserving their Native American Indian identity. I am proud of their determination, strength, and courage. I am overwhelmed and honored to have learned about their lives.

Many native peoples here in the United States and in Canada were treated as a lower class of people by their nations' governments and by non-Indian settlers moving onto their lands. Recently, Canadian Indian tribes started sharing their true stories of discrimination and subjugation, telling the world of their forced assimilation into white culture by the Canadian government. Canadian Indians (including some Oneida who moved to Canada after being forced to leave their homeland in New York State), shared what happened to them at Canadian Indian boarding schools and on Canadian Indian reservations. I am so glad that they've had the courage to share their stories of forced assimilation, physical and mental brutality, sexual abuse, and even murder for the sake of making their tribes' lands available for non-Indian settlers. I am sure it was extremely painful for them to share such stories of atrocities, but they have been courageous to do so. I was shocked to learn about what happened to the Canadian Indians, including some members of my own Oneida tribe.

In 2007 the Canadian government issued a public apology to all Canadian Indians for the atrocities they had suffered. The Canadian government showed real class, conscience, and guts to make this honest apology, and I was very surprised but happy to hear it.

During my thirteen years of research, I was shocked to learn about the mistreatment Elizabeth and Sophia suffered at a boarding school and the Oneida Reservation right here in America. Learning how the US government tried to handle its "Indian problem" by setting up boarding schools to assimilate Indian children into white culture has been very painful for me, and so has learning that Native American Indians were herded like cattle onto reservations while their homelands were given away to non-Indian settlers. Watching the way Indians were falsely portrayed on television and in Hollywood movies made me not want to be Indian. My Oneida elders were forbidden to pass down my culture and language so that the Indian in me would be killed. Now I understand why I didn't know I was Native American Indian for years. I was colonized—raised white. I tried to act as much like the whites around me as I could so that I would be accepted. Deep down inside, I was ashamed to be Native American Indian. At one point in my life, I was actually prejudiced against myself! Sometimes I'd look in the mirror and wonder just who or what I was. To learn that I was Oneida was no big deal, but just what was an Oneida?

I have marveled at the fact that my husband, Chick, can comfortably and proudly share his Italian culture with everyone. He makes a mean dish of lasagna and meatballs, and our two sons and I just love to come home to eat it. This food is part of his family's culture, and his delicious Italian cooking inspires me to cook a real Oneida Indian dinner for my family.

I have felt sad that I couldn't share my Oneida heritage with my sons, my husband, or anyone because Sophia and Elizabeth were not allowed to share their culture with their children or grandchildren. But now that I have learned about these two ladies, I am determined to share my knowledge of my Oneida heritage with everyone! I truly thank God, our Creator, that I researched these two Oneida women's lives for thirteen years. I never thought that seeing Elizabeth's picture in a museum or hearing relatives say, "Sophia attended Carlisle," would ever result in such a journey of discovery.

If Richard Henry Pratt were alive today, I would tell him that he hasn't killed the Indian in me. Today, I don't fear repercussions from the government for learning about my Oneida culture and language, and I do not fear punishment for sharing this stain in American History with you. This story would not have been possible without learning about Sophia's and Elizabeth's determination and courage to keep their culture and language alive. I sincerely hope in my heart that the US government, like the Canadian government, has the strength to honestly apologize for the atrocities Sophia, Elizabeth, and all indigenous tribes here in the United States of America have suffered. Who knows if that apology will ever come?

I share this story because many people in America do not know about the forced assimilation of native peoples into white culture right here in our own country; are in denial about it; or are too hurt or scared to share their stories. It has hurt me to learn about what happened to Great-Grandma Sophia and Great-Great-Grandmother Elizabeth Huff and other relatives, including Grandma Millie. However, sharing this story with you has lifted a load off my shoulders and has freed me to be the Oneida Indian that I really am. Thank you for reading this book.

Epilogue

Except for a few years, I have lived in Wisconsin all my life. I am happy here, although winters can be challenging. The winter of 2013 to 2014 was one for the record books with fifty-nine days of temperatures at zero degrees or below and plenty of snow. But I love the seasons, and this is part of life.

Hanging in the closet are my favorite winter coat, hat, and mittens; I'd be lost without them. Then I recall that Elizabeth Huff had only a shawl around her and a scarf on her head when she stood outside in the snow in that iconic picture of the old Indian woman, my great-great-grandmother. Today I still want to give her my favorite winter coat, hat, and mittens so she can be warm.

I have been blessed in many ways. My husband, family and I are healthy. I know where my next meal will come from, and no one threatens to take my children from my husband and me. I also have freedom to explore my Oneida heritage without retribution.

Every year, I drive with my husband from our Wisconsin home to visit his family and friends out east. Our trip takes us along the Pennsylvania Turnpike past Carlisle, Pennsylvania. My great-grandmother Sophia took this same journey when she was fourteen and a half years old, not knowing what to expect or when she would see her family again. It's strange for me to drive on the same path she did more than one hundred years ago.

While in New Jersey, we stop to visit with Barb Smith and her son Geoff in their stately old Victorian home. We also visit the Johnson family living in the same house that Sophia spent ten years of her young life as a servant. I savor every moment of our visit. My heart fills with gratitude for having the opportunity to meet these wonderful people who helped to bring Sophia into my life. I also have much gratitude to my relatives for sharing stories about Sophia and Elizabeth so I could learn about them.

At times I wonder if I could have endured the hardships that these two women faced, standing up to racism with such dignity and grace. My husband, Chick, says I have their grit and determination. Maybe I do. One thing that I know for certain is I am now proud to be Oneida, a descendant of Sophia and Elizabeth. It's been a long time coming. I will never stop learning about my Oneida heritage. This is part of me.

Notes

1. David Wallace Adams, Education For Extinction (Lawrence, KS: University Press of Kansas, 1995), 21.

2. Adams, Education For Extinction, 51-59.

3. Nicholas Reynolds, A General History of the Oneida Nation of Wisconsin (Oneida, WI: Oneida Printing Office, 2010), pg. V.

4. Alex Haley, Roots (New York, NY: Vanguard Press, 1976), 8

5. Reynolds, A General History of the Oneida Nation of Wisconsin, pg. V.

6. Ibid., 18-19.

7. Jen Miller, Fry Bread, Smithsonian Magazine, July, 2008, article 79191, http://www.smithsonianmag.com/arts.cultural/frybread-79191.

8. Marriage record of Elizabeth Hill and Nicholas Huff, 1866. http://www.familytreemaker.geneology.com/users/c/h/u/richard-church-w/wesite.0001/u

9. Adams, Education for Extinction, 20.

10. Herbert S. Lewis, L. Gordon McLester III, Oneida Lives (Lincoln, NE: University of Nebraska Press, 2005), 150.

11. Barb Landis, Carlisle Indian School Researcher, Carlisle, PA.

12. History.com Staff, Japanese-American Relocation, 2009. www.history.com/topics/worldwar-ii/japanese-american-relocation

13. Adams, Education for Extinction, 108-109.

14. Ibid., 63.

15. Linda F. Witmer, The Indian Industrial School, (Carlisle, PA: Published by Cumberland County Historical Society, 1993), 23.

16. Witmer, The Indian Industrial School, 111-116.

17. Mark O. Hagenbuch, Richard Henry Pratt, The Carlisle Indian Industrial School U.S. Policies Related to American Indian Education 1879-1904, (PhD Diss., The Pennsylvania State University, 1998), 83.

18. Adams, Education for Extinction, 157-159

19. Ibid.

20. Barb Landis, Carlisle Indian School Researcher, Carlisle, PA.

21. Adams, Education for Extinction, 130-131.

22. Susan Shown Harjo, Bush in the field of Screams, NBC News,2004, US News-Life-Race & Diversity, http://www.nbcnews.com/id/5086u9/ns/us-news-life/t/bush-field-screams. Article discusses Carlisle School Cemetery.

23. U.S. Army Heritage and Education Center, Digital Collections: CIIS RG 99 RED ALBUM 1, #55. www.carlisle.army.mil/ahec/index.cfm U.S. Army Signal Corps Photographs. Article discusses Carlisle Indian School Graveyard being relocated. The bottom of this photo reads: "Bodies of Indians removed to this new site to make room for a new road."

24. Genevieve Bell, Telling Stories out of School. (PhD. Diss., Stanford University, 1998), 390-391.

25. Kay Porterfield, Brainwashing and Boarding Schools: Undoing the Shameful Legacy. http://www.kporterfield.com/aigttw/articles/boardingschool.html 1.

26. Hessian Guardhouse-Lobby Wall Inscription.

27. Jacqueline Fear-Segal, White Man's Club, (Lincoln, NE: University of Nebraska Press, 2007), 206-230.

28. Biography.com Editors, Tokyo Rose, 2000, A&E Television. http://www.biography.com/people/tokyo_rose_37481

29. Hagenbuch, Richard Henry Pratt, The Carlisle Indian Industrial School... (1998 thesis), 83.

30. National Archives and Records Administration Building, (Washington, D.C.), Carlisle Indian School Records of Grace Thumbo-NARA Record # 2559

31. Judith Jourdan, Edited by Jill McNutt, Article, "Salt Pork Avenue Project," Oneida, WI, 1992.

32. Adams, Education for Extinction, 17.

33. Richard Powless and Graduates of Hampton in 1888, Access Genealogy, http://www.accessgenealogy.com/native/schools/hampton2/ graduating class 1888htm.

34. Ibid.

35. Map of 1917 showing land allotments for Hyson and Richard Powless, Oneida, WI, Osbourne Road. www.ancestry.com

36. Luther Standing Bear Quote, (1933), http://www.humboldt.edu/~gol/kellogs/ boardingschools.html 15.

37. Our Spirits Don't Speak English: Indian Boarding School, DVD, Rich Heape Films, (2008), Dallas, TX, Bill Wright-Pattwin Indian interview.

38. Robert Ritzenhaler, Oneida Indians of Wisconsin, (Bulletin, Vol. 19, Milwaukee Public Museum, 1950. 14-15.

39. Ritzenhaler, Oneida Indians of Wisconsin, 18-20.